B-MOVIE NIGHT:

EIGHT PLAYS OF PURE EXPLOITATION

LARVA!

BIRDS IN A CAGE

COLD WAR

WORSTEST MOVIE EVER

Raise Your Hand... FROM THE DEAD!

HOW TO BE ATTRACTIVE

SLAVES OF THE BEAN

LADY KILLERS

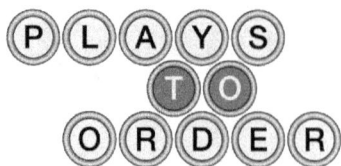

A Plays to Order collection
Published by Plays To Order
5724 Hollywood Blvd., Suite 109
Los Angeles, CA 90028
www.playstoorder.com

© 2016, 2017 Sean Abley, Kelly Goodman, Greg Machlin, Nathan Wellman, Natalie Nicole Dressel, Amy Seeley, Adam Hahn, Megan Gogerty

First Edition: March 2017

ISBN-13: 978-0998417318
ISBN-10: 0998417319

Cover design: Sean Abley

SkyPilot Theatre Company presents:

B-MOVIE NIGHT:

EIGHT PLAYS OF PURE EXPLOITATION

Written by

SEAN ABLEY

KELLY GOODMAN

GREG MACHLIN

NATHAN WELLMAN

NATALIE NICOLE DRESSEL

AMY SEELEY

ADAM HAHN

MEGAN GOGERTY

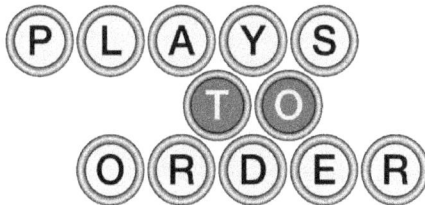

PLAYS TO ORDER

ACKNOWLEDGEMENTS

Thanks to SkyPilot Theatre Company in Los Angeles for being excited by the idea of a night of exploitation theater; The Playwrights Lab at Hollins University and Mill Mountain Theatre's Overnight Sensations for Megan Gogerty's prompts; and to B-movie filmmakers and their films for the inspiration.

TABLE OF CONTENTS

FOREWORD

One of my first contributions to SkyPilot Theatre was the idea of a B-movie night on stage as a fundraiser. SkyPilot is a membership company (a uniquely Los Angeles phenomenon where actors pay monthly dues after being accepted into the ensemble), and after an abbreviated season we needed a way to get everyone on stage. We also needed money, because SPT is a live theater production company and needing money is what live theater production companies do best.

Many moons ago, during The Bronze Age, I cofounded the Factory Theater in Chicago (still going strong 25 years later as of this writing), and although it wasn't our mission statement, or even a plan, movie styles on stage became one of our early trademarks. There's something about translating cinema conventions for the stage in a "theater for $5" way that makes me extremely happy, and our audiences agreed. I like to think we paved the way for shows like *The 39 Steps*, which so aped the Factory's style, when I saw it in London I had a moment of, "Is the West End ripping us off?" (Spoiler: they totally were.)

"Night of the Living Fundraiser" was a big success, bringing in some nice cashola, uniting the company for a fun night of work, and most importantly making the audience laugh. The evening was just six 10-minute(ish) plays by design (we needed time for the raffle), but when it came time to put this collection together I realized most theaters would need a bit more material for a full production. So I reached out to Megan Gogerty, my awesome professor from The Playwrights Lab at Hollins University, for her slasher satire *Lady Killers*, which had premiered at Overnight Sensations at Mill Mountain Theatre in Roanoke, VA; and my friend Amy Seeley, frequent collaborator and cofounder of the Factory Theatre, for her original piece *How to Be Attractive!*

Stay tuned for *B-Movie Night 2: Electric Boogaloo*!

Sean Abley
Dramaturg / Literary Manager, SkyPilot Theatre Company

ABOUT SKYPILOT THEATRE

SkyPilot Theatre Company is very proud to have produced "Night of the Living Fundraiser: A Tribute to B-Movies," now collected in this compilation as *B-Movie Night: Eight Plays of Pure Exploitation.* This night of original work fit right in with what SkyPilot has been doing since 2010—supporting our Playwrights' Wing and fulfilling our mission of producing provocative, compelling, and challenging new plays for the Los Angeles theater-going audience.

I'm very excited to see our resident playwrights' work, not only in print, but given more opportunities to be brought to life on stages throughout the country.

Shelby Janes
Board President, SkyPilot Theatre Company

PRODUCTION NOTES

When performed end-to-end, *B-Movie Night: Eight Plays of Pure Exploitation* is about 90 minutes without intermission. Each play is self-contained, so they may be broken out for one-act festivals or educational competitions for a reduced one-act royalty rate.

Companies mounting full productions may also want to add a horror host character between each play to create a themed evening (the audience is watching late-night *Chiller Theater* on television, attending a film festival, etc). If this is the case, the writer of the horror host's dialogue should be credited appropriately on the poster and in the program alongside the eight playwrights.

Full productions must use *B-Movie Night: Eight Plays of Pure Exploitation* as the title, and may include the names of each individual play as well (which we recommend. Who wouldn't want to see a play called *LARVA!*?) If produced separately, individual titles should be used instead.

And finally—as presented here, the plays are in the original production order, with *Lady Killers* and *How to Be Attractive!* dropped in with an eye toward a strong running order. Feel free to reorder the plays to suit your production's needs.

LARVA!

By Sean Abley

PLAYWRIGHT'S BIO

SEAN ABLEY is an award-winning playwright, screenwriter, novelist, and journalist. He has over thirty plays published by Plays to Order. Playscripts, Brooklyn Publishers, Heuer Publishing, Next Stage Press, and Eldridge Plays and Musicals, with titles like *End of the World (With Prom to Follow)*, *The Adventures of Rose Red (Snow White's Less-Famous Sister)*, *Horror High: The Musical* and *Attack of the Killer B's*. His television writing includes multiple episodes of *So Weird* (Disney Channel), *Sabrina, the Animated Series* (Disney/UPN), *Digimon* (Fox Family), as well as several pilots including *Bench Pressly, The World's Strongest Private Dick* with Ahmet Zappa, starring Bruce Campbell. Produced screenplays include the B-movies *Socket*, *Witchcraft 15: Blood Rose* and *Witchcraft 16: Hollywood Coven*. He was one on the founders of Chicago's prolific Factory Theater in 1992 (still going strong as of this writing), and the creator of the "Gay of the Dead" blog on Fangoria.com. His first novel, a new novelization of *Night of the Living Dead*, was recently published by Dark Blue Things.

SYNOPSIS

Before there was The Fly, there was...

In this B-movie on stage, a combination of an earthquake, a tornado, and a lightning strike on a nuclear power plant, brings super smart nuclear larva to Villagetown. Dr. Charlotte Wilson and Sheriff O'Reilly must stop the infestation of the aggressive maggots, but not before Dr. Wilson is made their queen.

SETTING

Mid-1970s. In and around a small, rural town in the Midwest.

PRODUCTION NOTES

The staging for the original production of *LARVA!* was purposefully low budget in look and feel. The entire set was two folding chairs which began as a car, then transformed into an autopsy table when covered with a white sheet. The autopsy table remained in place for the rest of the play, with lighting utilized to create different locations on other areas of the stage.

The practical special effects were, for the most part, executed by an on-stage actor dressed in all black. When larva attacks were called for, this actor would dump bucketfuls of green styrofoam packing peanuts onto the actors in full view. The mountain in the distance was a crude drawing on poster board, taped to the wall when called for. When the Mayor climbed the mountain the black-clad actor manipulated a doll in an identical costume; ditto the swarm of nuclear flies attaching themselves to the giant no-pest strips. You get the idea—theater for $5. Be creative... and cheap!

<u>CHARACTERS</u>

CHARLOTTE WILSON (f)	30s-50s, beautiful and brainy regardless of age. A lady assistant coroner with dreams of being a full-fledged coroner.
SHERIFF O'REILLY (m)	40s-50s, ruggedly handsome. Been sheriff around these parts for a decade or more.
DR. DOYLE (m)	50s-70s cranky old man who happens to be the coroner.
BRENDA (f)	20s, horny young woman.
CHUCK (m)	20s, horny young man.
MAYOR MILLER (f)	Any age, a small town mayor concerned with the town's bottom line.

MOM (f)

EMCEE (m/f)

BEAUTY QUEEN (f)

DOCTOR (m/f)

NURSE (m/f)

PAGEANT CONTESTANT (f)

ON-STAGE EFFECTS (m/f)

SUGGESTED DOUBLING (with some roles in drag):

- BRENDA / MAYOR MILLER / BEAUTY QUEEN
- DR. DOYLE / PAGEANT CONTESTANT / NURSE
- CHUCK / EMCEE / MOM / DOCTOR

ACKNOWLEDGEMENTS

LARVA! was first performed as part of SkyPilot Theatre's "Night of the Living Fundraiser" on September 17, 2016 at the Pan Andreas Theatre in Los Angeles, CA. The production was directed by Sean Abley. The cast was as follows:

Tina Walsch	...................................Charlotte Wilson, MD
Brad Griffith	...…………………………..Sheriff O'Reilly
Jim Blanchette	........Dr. Doyle / Nurse / Pageant Contestant
Dwana White	......Brenda / Mayor Miller / Beauty Queen
Ian Nemser	...............Chuck / Emcee / Mom / Doctor
Sean Abley	.…………………………...On-Stage Effects

LARVA!

By Sean Abley

SCENE ONE

(*CAR IN A SECLUDED SPOT IN A RURAL AREA. We hear SFX: Thunder, rain and wind. CHUCK, a horny young man in his 20s, and BRENDA, a horny young woman in her 20s, make out in her car. Mid-1970s classic rock plays on the radio.*)

BRENDA. Chuck, we need to get out of this rainstorm! That lightning is really close!

CHUCK. Brenda, a car is the safest place to be in a lightning storm. Even if the lightning hits the car, we're grounded by the rubber tires. We'll be fine. Let's get back to your boobs.

(*SFX: Loud thunder. BRENDA jumps.*)

BRENDA. Did you see that?! Lightning just hit the nuclear power plant!

CHUCK. Brenda, a nuclear power plant is the safest place to be in a lightning storm. That's a government facility. They're prepared for any acts of nature. We'll be fine. Really, let's get back to your boobs.

(*SFX: Earthquake rumble. The car shakes.*)

BRENDA. Chuck, did you feel that?! It's an earthquake.

CHUCK. Brenda, I really need you to concentrate on showing me your boobs.

(*SFX: Tornado approaching.*)

BRENDA. Chuck, do you see that?! It's a tornado!

CHUCK. Brenda—

(*The ON-STAGE EFFECTS actor pours enlarged green larva into the car onto CHUCK and BRENDA. The larva attack. SFX: larva attack.*)

CHUCK. Oh, my God! What is it?!

BRENDA. They look like larva! Larvas? Larvae? A bunch of larvas!

CHUCK. Gaaaahhhh!!! They're eating me alive! Help! Brenda, help me! Your boooooobs....

(CHUCK and BRENDA panic as the larvae attack and the tornado moves closer. BLACKOUT. In the dark we hear MUSIC: 1970s Horror Film Opening Credits music.)

SCENE TWO

(MORGUE. CHARLOTTE WILSON, M.D., a beautiful and smart assistant coroner who does everything sexily; SHERIFF O'REILLY, a ruggedly handsome man of the law; and DR. DOYLE, a cranky old coroner, examine a body under a sheet.)

DR. DOYLE. Well, it's a mystery to me. I can't figure out what killed this boy. He appears to have been eaten by something small but for the life of me I can't figure out what.

SHERIFF. Doctor, there must be some explanation. This kid isn't even from Villagetown. His I.D. says he's from Cityville, two counties away.

CHARLOTTE. Cityville?

DR. DOYLE. Now Charlotte...

SHERIFF. That's right. His car was found overturned in downtown Villagetown last night. His girl Brenda was in the passenger seat, unconscious but alive... and pregnant!

CHARLOTTE. So that could mean...

DR. DOYLE. Charlotte, please. Don't go off on one of your wild theories. That's of no help here.

SHERIFF. Wild theories is all we have at the moment, Doc. Let's hear it, Dr. Wilson.

CHARLOTTE. *(Sexily.)* Well, these chew marks appear to be from some sort of larger than normal maggot. Last night there was a storm in Cityville, and news reports about lightning hitting the nuclear power plant. What if the strike released nuclear waste into the ground, transforming normal larvae into super larva? Then the subsequent earthquake opened a crack in the ground, releasing the larvae from deep in the earth to attack this young couple. And then the tornado carried their car all the way to Villagetown.

DR. DOYLE. Well, that's ridiculous!

SHERIFF. Not so fast, Doc. I think she's on to something. Doctor—

CHARLOTTE. Sheriff, you've known me since I was a teenager. You can call me Charlotte.

SHERIFF. Charlotte. If what you say is true, what's the next step?

CHARLOTTE. Well, I can guarantee there are more larvae out there. We need to study them and figure out how to eradicate them from the area.

(MAYOR MILLER, a lady mayor, enters. She is wearing a beauty pageant sash and tiara. Perhaps she enters with a little musical fanfare as she smiles and waves at the nonexistent crowd.)

MAYOR. Hello, everyone!

CHARLOTTE / SHERIFF / DR. DOYLE. *(Grudgingly.)* Hello, Mayor Miller...

MAYOR. So, have we figured out what killed our young lothario here?

SHERIFF. Doctor Wilson here has a theory.

DR. DOYLE. And it's bunk! Listen to me, young lady. You're never going to be a full coroner in Villagetown if you keep spinning ridiculous tales about larva and tornadoes.

(DR. DOYLE exits.)

MAYOR. Larva?

(DR. DOYLE reenters.)

DR. DOYLE. And tornadoes!

(DR. DOYLE exits.)

CHARLOTTE. Giant nuclear radiated larvae.

MAYOR. More than one?

CHARLOTTE. Thousands of them!

MAYOR. Eiiew. Goodbye!

(*MAYOR moves to exit.*)

CHARLOTTE. Wait! We have to warn the town!

MAYOR. Warn the town to be on the lookout for giant radiated larva? And what do you think that will do for the crowds at the 23rd Annual Little Miss Squash Blossom Pageant and Hog Tie? As the first crowned winner of the Little Miss Squash Blossom Pageant, and first runner up for the Hog Tie, I'm not going to shut down this town's third most important event on some larval theory, Dr. Wilson. You destroy those larvas and keep this quiet or you'll be fishing dead bodies out of the ponds down at Lakestream River. (*Abrupt change.*) Goodbye everyone!

(*MAYOR smiles and waves as she exits. Perhaps a musical play off?*)

CHARLOTTE. Sheriff, what are we going to do? Even if Dr. Doyle will allow me to research how to stop the larvae, the pageant and hog tie are next week. (*Disproportionate hysteria.*) I need more time! I need more time!

(*SHERIFF grabs her in a vaguely affectionate way, rubbing her shoulders to calm her down.*)

SHERIFF. Calm down, Charlotte

CHARLOTTE. I'm sorry, Sheriff.

SHERIFF. I've known you since you were a teenager and I was your late father's best friend. Call me Bud.

CHARLOTTE. Bud.

SHERIFF. If Dr. Doyle gives you any guff, I'll handle him. You just concentrate on what you need to do to stop those larva. Got it?

CHARLOTTE. Yes, Bud.

(*They don't kiss, but they sure want to.*

LIGHTS SHIFT to—)

SCENE THREE

(*LARVA DEATH MONTAGE. SFX: Horror movie music and stings underneath.*

ON AN OUTDOOR STAGE. A EMCEE announces a pageant winner as BEAUTY QUEEN and PAGEANT CONTESTANT nervously await the results.)

EMCEE. And the winner of the 1978 Little Miss Squash Blossom pageant is... Miss Amber Cupcinette, you're the new Little Miss Squash Blossom 1978!

(*PAGEANT CONTESTANT exits as EMCEE crowns BEAUTY QUEEN. ON-STAGE EFFECTS actor dumps larvae on them. The scream in horror as they exit.*

DR. DOYLE'S HOME. He is snacking on cheese puffs.)

DR. DOYLE. Nuclear larva my ass...

(*DR. DOYLE turns the cheese puffs container up to pour the puffs into his mouth. Larva pour out instead, covering his face and eating his flesh.*)

DR. DOYLE. Gaaaahhhh!!!!!

(*He screams and exits.*

CHILD'S BEDROOM. MOM sets down a bassinet with a baby in it.)

MOM. There you go. Bottle time!

(*MOM turns to retrieve bottle. While her back is turned, ON-STAGE EFFECTS actor pours larva into the bassinet. MOM returns.*)

MOM. Here you go! (*Sees baby covered in larva, screams.*) Gaaaahhh!!!

(*MOM pulls baby out of bassinet—it is a baby's body with a bare skull for a head. She screams and exits.*

LIGHTS SHIFT to—)

SCENE FOUR

(*MORGUE. CHARLOTTE and the MAYOR.*)

MAYOR. I have some good news! I'm promoting you to head coroner of Villagetown!
CHARLOTTE. Thank you, Mayor! This is an incredible honor!
MAYOR. (*Gestures to the body covered by a sheet.*) And your first duty as head coroner will be to examine the body of your former boss, Dr. Doyle. Enjoy!

(*MAYOR exits. CHARLOTTE examines the body. She pulls a dead larva from the corpse.*)

CHARLOTTE. Gotcha! Well, well, well. Hello Mr. Fly Larva. Now how did you get so big...

(*As she works we hear SFX: larva scrambling around. ON-STAGE EFFECTS actor attaches larva to the wall. When CHARLOTTE finally hears them, she turns around to find larva have spelled out "OUR QUEEN" on the wall.*)

CHARLOTTE. (*Screaming.*) Aaaahhhh!!!

(*ON-STAGE EFFECTS actor dumps larvae on her. As she sexily bats them away and screams, SHERIFF enters, gun drawn. He aims and methodically fires his gun at each larva on the floor, killing them. Maybe there are so many he has to reload. This should take a comically long time. When he's finally finished he grabs CHARLOTTE.*)

SHERIFF. Are you okay?!
CHARLOTTE. I am now. Did you see their message on the wall?
SHERIFF. "Our queen." What does that mean?

CHARLOTTE. I don't know, but what I do know is these are super smart fly larva, also known as maggots. My guess is they've developed a higher intelligence courtesy of the nuclear radiation. Right now they're in the pupa stage, but they'll transform to flies soon, and they may be harder to stop than we thought.

SHERIFF. Damn that nuclear power plant.

CHARLOTTE. Oh, Bud, did you see how they attacked me? I can still feel them, crawling all over me! I can hear them. I can hear them think!

SHERIFF. Can you hear me think? Like a man?

(SHERIFF kisses her, and they make sweet love in the morgue. [NOTE: The original production used the white sheet from the corpse, two dolls and a flashlight to create a "Making Love Shadow Play" for this moment.]

LIGHTS SHIFT to—)

SCENE FIVE

(MORGUE. LATER. SFX: larva rustling around, calling out to CHARLOTTE.)

LARVAE. (*Unintelligible bug noises.*)

(While SHERIFF sleeps, CHARLOTTE awakes with a start at the sound.)

CHARLOTTE. (*In a trance.*) Yes... yes... yes, I will lead you... I will lead you!! Come to me! Bow down before me as I am your queen!!

(SFX: larva noise gradually changing into fly buzzing. SHERIFF wakes up to find CHARLOTTE transforming into a human fly queen.)

SHERIFF. Charlotte! What's happening to you?!

CHARLOTTE. (*Lady fly voice.*) I ammmm transformmmming...I ammm becoming a great leeeeaderrrr.... I ammmmm the queeeennnn....

(*CHARLOTTE encroaches on SHERIFF.*)

SHERIFF. Stay back!
CHARLOTTE. Beee my mmmmate, Ssshhhhheriff.... Mmmmmmate with mmmmmeeee!!
SHERIFF. Charlotte, stop!
CHARLOTTE. Donnnnn't you like mmmmeee? Donnn't you finnnnd mmmmeeee attraaaactivvvvve?
SHERIFF. My God, you're hideous!

(*MAYOR enters.*)

MAYOR. Any chance you've finished that autopsy HOLY MARY MOTHER OF GOD!!!

(*SHERIFF pulls MAYOR aside.*)

MAYOR. What's happened to her?
SHERIFF. She's been infected by the nuclear larva. She's transforming to their final stage, a human fly.
MAYOR. What do we do?
SHERIFF. I have an idea.

(*SHERIFF's long explanation, complete with mime action, is drowned out by fly buzzing.*)

SHERIFF. ... and save the town!
MAYOR. Are you sure it will work.
SHERIFF. It has to! Get going!

(*MAYOR rushes out.*)

CHARLOTTE. Wheeere is sssssheee going?
SHERIFF. She's going to get you some nice garbage to eat. Wouldn't that be nice?
CHARLOTTE. Ohhhh, Buuuud. Youuuu thinnnnnk of everrrrry thinnnnggg.

(*SHERIFF grimaces, then moves in and tenderly holds CHARLOTTE.*)

SHERIFF. Charlotte, darling... I know you're still in there. I know you are. Can you speak to me, Charlotte? Can you talk to me one last time before you transform completely?

CHARLOTTE. (*Struggling to speak normally.*) Bud.... Oh, Bud... (*Cries.*) I'm so sorry. I've really messed things up, haven't I?

SHERIFF. No, no. Shhhh, don't say that. But I need you to do something for me. For me and the entire town.

CHARLOTTE. Anything...

SHERIFF. Do you see out the window, way up on the side of the mountain? That's the mayor up there.

(*SPLIT SCENE - A MINIATURE MOUNTAIN SET slides in via the ON-STAGE EFFECTS actor, representing the mountain in the distance. We see a miniature MAYOR there as well, attaching giant no-pest strips to the mountains.*)

CHARLOTTE. What's she doing? What are those huge pieces of paper for?

SHERIFF. Those are industrial size no-pest strips. I asked her to put them up there.

CHARLOTTE. No... (*Cries.*)

SHERIFF. I need you to fly up there, lead your nuclear super smart fly swarm into those strips. Save the town, Charlotte. Be the head coroner mutant lady fly I know you can be.

CHARLOTTE. Oh, Bud...

(*CHARLOTTE and SHERIFF kiss passionately.*)

CHARLOTTE. Goodbye, Bud. I'll always love you...

(*CHARLOTTE flies away, exiting the stage. SFX: flies buzzing, swarming, following her.*

On the MOUNTAIN MINIATURE SET, we see a mini CHARLOTTE fly in via the ON-STAGE EFFECTS actor, and finally stick to the no-pest strip. Then a swarm of flies follows. SFX: fly death.)

SHERIFF. She did it! My God, she did it!

(*An unseen crowd cheers. SFX: crowd cheering.*

LIGHTS SHIFT to—)

SCENE SIX

(*DELIVERY ROOM. BRENDA is on the delivery table. A DOCTOR and NURSE are coaxing her through labor.*)

DOCTOR. Okay Brenda, breathe, breathe, deep breaths...
BRENDA. Oh, God, I can't! I can't!

(*BRENDA starts convulsing.*)

DOCTOR. Oh, my God! My God...
NURSE. Doctor! What's happening?!

(*BRENDA's stomach bursts open, spewing larva everywhere. BLACKOUT. SFX: end of horror movie sting and credits music.*)

END OF PLAY

BIRDS IN A CAGE

By Kelly Goodman

PLAYWRIGHT'S BIO

KELLY GOODMAN has been writing, acting and doing comedy for most of her life. She starred at 4 years old as the "Queen Who Hated Spring" and hasn't looked back. Kelly is a headlining performer and improv teacher and has performed stand-up, sketch, and improv comedy all over the country including The Hollywood Improv, The Comedy Store, ACME and Second City in Chicago.

SYNOPSIS

An homage to "girls behind bars films" such as *Caged* and *Switchblade Sisters*, *Birds in a Cage* is the story of hardened criminal, Big Mama, and the daughter she left behind when she was sent up the river. When it comes to the mother-daughter bond, Big Mama will stop at nothing to be with her little girl, Eugenia...FOREVER!

SETTING

1950's Women's House of Detention, Ephemeral NY

CHARACTERS

BIG MAMA (f)   Hardened criminal, the queen of the cell block.

BUTTERCUP (f)   Innocent-like inmate, MAMA's pet.

HANK (m)   Prison guard. Young handsome, on the take but, still a tad naïve.

EUGENIA (f)   MAMA's long lost daughter, thinks she can save the world.

ACKNOWLEDGEMENTS

Birds in a Cage was first performed as part of SkyPilot Theatre's "Night of the Living Fundraiser" on September 17, 2016 at the Pan Andreas Theatre in Los Angeles, CA. The production was directed by Lois Winer Weiss. The cast was as follows:

Kelly Goodman   ....Big Mama
Sarah Marcum   ....Buttercup
Marie Pettit   ....Eugenia
Duane Taniguchi   ....Officer O'Hanahan

BIRDS IN A CAGE

By Kelly Goodman

(*THE PRISON COMMON ROOM. LIGHTS COME UP as BIG MAMA and BUTTERCUP are playing cards...they are both staring intently at their cards...*)

MAMA. Hey, bird brain...ya gonna take your turn or what?

BUTTERCUP. Yeah... I'm just... hmmmmmm, this is just so hard...

MAMA. What's so hard... fer Chrissakes just take yer turn!

BUTTERCUP. Okay, okay... jeez... ummmm... okay... you got any threes?

MAMA. (*Handing over a bunch of cards.*) Ahhhh, crap... ya got me Buttercup, you got me good this time!

BUTTERCUP. (*Giggling.*) YAY! You gotta pay up now...fair and square...you said the best 78 out of 143... I won... I won (*Sing-songy.*) I wonnnn now gimme my Twinkies!

MAMA. Alright, alright...shut yer trap. Here ya go...

(*MAMA reaches into her cleavage and hands BUTTERCUP a package of Twinkies.*)

MAMA. ... fair and square... now don't go eating them all at once, ya hear me... you have no idea what I had to do to get those.

BUTTERCUP. Oooooh, did you have to perform various and sundry undesirable sex acts on a prison guard?

MAMA. Noooooo...

BUTTERCUP. Oooooh, did you have to decapitate Old Sadie from the commissary?

MAMA. Noooo... actually I....

BUTTERCUP. Oooooh, did you have one of you outside goons highjack a Hostess truck and sneak you in the goods in his pants on visiting day?

MAMA. Noooo...okay, I just reached my hand up under the vending machine... (*BUTTERCUP is clearly disappointed.*)... but, my hand coulda got stuck... I mean, I coulda bled to death or got gangrene or something... it wasn't that easy... anyway...

that's not the point... just don't eat 'em all at once... now shuffle the cards.

(*HANK the prison guard enters... he comes over to the table...*)

HANK. How're my two favorite jailbirds doin' this fine evening? (*Tips his hat.*) Big Mama? And the lovely Miss Buttercup? (*He is clearly smitten with BUTTERCUP.*)

BUTTERCUP. Good evening officer O'Hannihan... that's a mighty handsome uniform you got on today! (*She is smitten right back.*)

HANK. (*Flirting.*) This old thing? It's the same thing I wear every day, Buttercup!

MAMA. Enough, you two... quit yer canoodling... hey Hank, ya got my goods?

(*HANK takes his hat off and pulls out a bottle of booze and some cigarettes.*)

HANK. Only the finest for you Big Mama...

MAMA. (*Gets some money out of her cleavage.*) Here ya go, kid...

HANK. (*Looks at bill with earnest amazement.*) Golly! Big Mama... thanks a bunch!

MAMA. You keep bringing me cigs and hooch and there are many more Abraham Lincolns in your future, kid!

HANK. I believe that is "Officer" Kid to you...

(*At this attempt at a joke, BUTTERCUP laughs a bit too hard and MAMA glares at him.*)

HANK. Ummmm, well at any rate... it's about 30 minutes till lock up, ladies... oh and it looks like you'll be getting a new cellmate this evening...

(*As he says this, EUGENIA enters carrying her bedding and new prisoner stuff.*)

HANK. ... Ah, speak of the devil.

BUTTERCUP. But, she ain't got no horns...

HANK. It's a figure of speech... uhhh, nevermind... 30 minutes, ladies.

(*HANK exits.*)

MAMA. Well, well, well... look what the cat drug in... you got a name Birdy?

EUGENIA. Uhhh, yes ma'am... it's Eugenia... are you the one they call Big Mama?

MAMA. I am... what's it to you? Eugenia, eh? I had a daughter named Eugenia... probably about your age... they took her away from me when I got sent up the river...

EUGENIA. Is that right?

BUTTERCUP. Wow, that's a coinky-dink for sure!

MAMA. Where you from, Birdy?

EUGENIA. Little Neck, Queens... ma'am.

MAMA. I'm from Little Neck, Queens...

EUGENIA. Is that right?

BUTTERCUP. WOW... another coinky-dink! AMAZING!

(*MAMA and EUGENIA pretty much ignore BUTTERCUP, each of them trying to figure out what the other woman is going to do as more information is revealed.*)

MAMA. Where are your parents, Birdy?

EUGENIA. I never knew my dad... and my mom got sent up the river when I was a little girl... I barely remember her... I do remember her name though, it was Cornelia May and I remember she used to sing to me a song about a woman from St Louie...

MAMA. My old man took off after our baby girl was born... went out for a half of pound of brussels sprouts and never came back... say, and my name is Cornelia May and I happen to know a song about a St Louie woman...

EUGENIA. Is that right...

BUTTERCUP. OH MY GOSH!!! (*They both turn to her to reveal what is painfully obvious.*) Your name is Cornelia May? Really? I had you pegged for more of a Betty or Sally...

MAMA. Shut yer trap Buttercup... (*To EUGENIA.*) You know what this means, right?

BUTTERCUP. (*Pleased with herself.*) It means that Eugenia probably knows your daughter!

EUGENIA / MAMA. Shut yer trap Buttercup!

MAMA. (*Putting her arms out to EUGENIA.*) Oh, my baby girl! Come here! (*They embrace.*) How did you find me?

EUGENIA. People on the street talk, ya hear things… I boosted a car just to come find you! They gave me 6 months to a year… so that will give me plenty of time to get you out of here, Mama! We can have a life together, it's not too late.

MAMA. Oh, Birdy… I ain't ever getting' outta here… I'm a lifer. Don't ya get it? These four walls are my home… I'll be in this cage till my dying day!

BUTTERCUP. Yup, till her dying day…

MAMA. Look Buttercup, I don't need you anymore… I have my real daughter here… scram, get lost… go see if Old Sadie in the commissary is looking for a surrogate daughter with subtle Sapphic subtext… Go on!

(*BUTTERCUP starts to cry and walk away dejectedly.*)

MAMA. Wait Buttercup…

(*BUTTERCUP hopefully stops in her tracks as MAMA pulls another pack of Twinkies from her cleavage…tosses them to her.*)

MAMA. I'll still need my laundry… easy on the starch, Kid!

BUTTERCUP. (*Delighted.*) YAY! (*Sing-songy.*) Easy on the starch…

(*BUTTERCUP skips off with clutching her Twinkies to her chest.*)

EUGENIA. Mama, I can get you outta here… I know I can. I've been taking night classes at the secretary school. I can write good letters… a letter to the warden, a letter to the governor, even the president if I have to. I found you now… (*Tearfully.*) I'm not going to lose you again!

MAMA. (*Holds out her arms again.*) Oh, Birdy… come here… (*Wipes at her tears.*) Don't cry Eugenia… there, that's better. I'm too far gone, Birdy… I'll never see light of day again. I've done some bad, bad… I mean REALLY bad things… I ain't proud of it… but, I accepted my fate years ago… it does my heart good that you boosted a car just to get in here to see me… real good. But, it ain't no use. I'm not going anywhere no matter how many letters you write. (*Hugs her one last time.*)

EUGENIA. Oh, mama…I love you so much!

MAMA. I love you too, Birdy! (*Yells offstage.*) HANK… you better get in here and pat this new Birdy down for contraband before lights out!

(*HANK runs onstage… pats EUGENIA down… he pulls a few ridiculously large bags of drugs, cash maybe cigarettes/booze, just keeps finding them on EUGENIA. EUGENIA can't believe it… she improvises some denials, "But, you just gave me these clothes… I didn't have this with me when I got here…" something like that… MAMA just sits back with a smirk on her face through this whole interaction.*)

HANK. (*Gathering up all the evidence.*) I gotta go show the warden… looks like you aren't going anywhere for a very, very, very long time little lady!

(*HANK exits.*)

EUGENIA. But, how… (*Looks at MAMA.*) You… you… planted all of that extremely bulky and illegal contraband on me while you were hugging me… didn't you? But, why mama? WHYYYY?

(*MAMA gathers her in an uncomfortable hug.*)

MAMA. Welcome to the cage, Birdy…

(*LIGHTS FADE on EUGENIA's horrified face as MAMA hums "St. Louie Woman."*)

END OF PLAY

COLD WAR

By Greg Machlin

PLAYWRIGHT'S BIO

GREG MACHLIN is a 2016 Nicholl Fellowship Semi-Finalist and Austin Semi-Finalist for his screenplay *7 Days: A Fantasia on the Life of Miles Davis*. A graduate of the University of Iowa's MFA Playwriting Workshop, Greg also wrote the sci-fi bio-play *Keith Haring: Pieces of a Life*, authorized by the Keith Haring estate, which enjoyed a sold-out run in L.A. As a digital series creator, he co-created *WRNG in Studio City* and was a writer-producer on *L.A. Beer*, the world's first multi-cam comedy digital series, which received a positive review from Variety and is available to stream at labeer.tv. Other full-length plays include the vampire romantic comedy *Bloody Lies* (MITF 2007, Best New Script Finalist) and *A History Of Bad Ideas* (Iowa New Play Festival, 2008). His one-acts include *Family Portrait* (Heideman Finalist, 2008) and *Smart Phone* (Theatre Unleashed, 2014), which authorities say may be the scariest ten-minute ever written.

SYNOPSIS

It's gonna get cold in here.

When killer snowmen invade the town of Waterville, California, certain members of the town desperately attempt to fight back—to no avail, because the town council is too focused on the upcoming turnip festival.

SETTING

At night, in the woods; in the lab of Dr. Scientist; at a town council meeting.

CHARACTERS

THE NARRATOR (m/f)	Sly and easily irritated.
DUANE / SNOWMAN (m)	Not that bright, but likeable.
ABBY (f)	The least evil snowman.
DR. SCIENTIST/ SNOWMAN #2 (m/f)	A decent sort, dedicated to science. / Addicted to Pokemon.
KRYSTAL (f)	Smart, but not smart enough to stop the snowmen.
SHELLY (f)	Able to wield power well.
LAWSON (m/f)	A reprehensible sellout.
JEROME (m)	Not detail-oriented enough.

PRODUCTION NOTES

This is a straight-up B-movie parody, so sets and costumes can literally be as poorly-constructed/cardboard as necessary. In fact, if there's anything you can't do, just give the stage direction to the Narrator as a line. That's part of what they're there for.

For the transformations into snowmen, it can be as simple as actors putting a carrot on their nose—or a carrot attached to sunglasses, which was Joe's and the cast's elegant solution.

For the scene in which SNOWMAN shows up disguised, in the L.A. production, the actor literally held a paper-plate face on a stick.

ACKNOWLEDGEMENTS

Cold War was first performed as part of SkyPilot Theatre's "Night of the Living Fundraiser" on September 17, 2016 at the Pan Andreas Theatre in Los Angeles, CA. The production was directed by Joe Luis Cedillo. The cast was as follows:

Marie Petit	The Narrator
Jude Evans	Duane / Snowman
Sarah Marcum	Abby
Duane Taniguchi	Dr. Scientist / Snowman #2
Patricia Mizen	Krystal
Catherine Cox	Shelly
Tina Walsch	Lawson
David Caprita	Jerome

COLD WAR

By Greg Machlin

(At LIGHTS UP we see a suggested forest. THE NARRATOR stands off to the side, looking delightfully stern, and addresses the audience.)

THE NARRATOR. The town of Waterville, California was like any other sleepy California town. Until that dreaded day in 2016 when the citizens learned the true meaning of the words "Cold War."

DUANE. Man, Abby, it sure was great to meet you today. Glad you suggested a night hike in the woods! I don't tend to meet many girls in the meat freezer at John's Grocery.

THE NARRATOR. It had not occurred to Duane to think that Abby's hours spent in the meat freezer were odd. Because—

DUANE. (*To audience.*) Abby's *hot!*

(Ominous howl of an animal.)

ABBY. (*Suddenly spooked.*) Are you sure we're alone out here?

DUANE. Yeah, it's totes deserted and mad quiet, just like you wanted. Don't worry, I'm not gonna kill you or anything! Ha, ha!

ABBY. (*Super-awkward laugh.*) Ha ha ha ha ha!

THE NARRATOR. Duane was weirded out by Abby's laugh. But also turned on.

DUANE. So… you want to make out?

ABBY. Duane, do you ever think about snow?

DUANE. Uhh. Like, from the sky, or cocaine?

ABBY. From the sky. Don't you think it's too hot out here in California? If it were colder, you could cuddle with someone under the blankets.

DUANE. Oh yeah!

ABBY. And if there were a giant dome covering Waterville, it'd be so cold you could cuddle with them all the time!

DUANE. Abby, is this how they talk dirty where you're from?

(*ABBY produces a sharp carrot.*)

ABBY. You see, once upon a time *SNOW MEN* ruled the earth. And then you humans took our land and made it much too hot! And we had to flee! It's the fault of you and all your kind!

DUANE. But I was totes respectful of your hot bod!

THE NARRATOR. Duane was *not* representative of all humankind.

(*ABBY'S posture changes. She expands and transforms into a snowman!*)

ABBY. We have been around since the Ice Age. We are *SNOW MEN.*

DUANE. Wow. Do all your parts get bigger when you expand? That's hot!

ABBY. *I HATE HOT!*

(*ABBY reaches back and accidentally stabs DUANE with her carrot.*)

DUANE. (*Gasping in pain.*) Aw man, *I* was supposed to be sticking something in *you.*

ABBY. (*Genuinely horrified.*) Oh no! You meant 'hot' as in attractive! Damn it, I totally would've enslaved you instead of killing you. Phallic objects are dangerous.

(*DUANE lets out a death gurgle and dies. ABBY makes a cooing noise and a snow dove appears. Probably just thrown onstage.*)

ABBY. (*To the bird.*) This town is perfect for us to infiltrate and build a dome over! They'll never see us coming! Tell my snow brothers and sisters to come to Waterville! The town is *made* of water!

(*ABBY throws the snow-dove offstage. Or, I don't know, maybe it flies.*)

THE NARRATOR. If only the town had been named Desert-ville.

(ABBY exits. B-Movie-esque HORROR MUSIC plays. The cast holds up cheesy movie-style credits signs, which read: "A LAB." "Saturday." "7:33." "PM.")

THE NARRATOR. Seriously? I was just about to say that!

(A lab. DR. SCIENTIST and KRYSTAL, a Ph.D. candidate, examine DUANE'S body.)

THE NARRATOR. In the lab. Part One: There's something suspicious about all these dead bodies.
DR. SCIENTIST. There's something suspicious about all these dead bodies!
THE NARRATOR. I *literally* just said that.
KRYSTAL. Dr. Scientist—
DR. SCIENTIST. That's not how it's pronounced!
KRYSTAL. *(Sighs.)* Dr. Skee-EN-ticed... people are showing up dead, with visible signs of hypothermia despite the heat, surrounded by snowflakes and drops of water. Except for Duane, with that weird hole in his body.
DR. SCIENTIST. What do you think it means, Krystal?
KRYSTAL. I hypothesize something cold and long plunged into him—
DR. SCIENTIST. No, the other corpsicles!
KRYSTAL. I think it means townspeople are getting killed by evil snowmen!
DR. SCIENTIST. Krystal, what have I told you about jumping to conclusions? We do not have enough data! For example, there are no eyewitness reports of snowmen killing townspeople.
KRYSTAL. Dr. Scientist, I really think we need to find ways to heat up the town!
DR. SCIENTIST. Nonsense! These are all clearly random deaths! If you start spreading these rumors, you'll ruin Waterville's prized turnip festival!
THE NARRATOR. Waterville had the best turnip festival in the nation, partially because no other town was particularly keen on turnips.
DR. SCIENTIST. Also, you're a woman, and therefore clearly inferior.

(*ABBY and another SNOWMAN runs into the lab.*)

SNOWMAN. Death to human scientists!
ABBY. (*To SNOWMAN.*) Uh, a bit much?
DR. SCIENTIST. No! Impossible! My lab is full of snow people!
ABBY. Snow men.
DR. SCIENTIST. You can't say 'snow men'!
ABBY. It's *our* species! We'll call ourselves whatever we want!

(*ABBY grabs DR. SCIENTIST and breathes on him, freezing him to death.*)

DR. SCIENTIST. No! Blood cooling! Body heat disappearing!
SNOWMAN. Now who's 'a little much'?
ABBY. Come on, you said 'death to all humans!'
KRYSTAL. You *monsters!*

(*KRYSTAL grabs a heavy object of some kind and chases the snow men out of the lab.*)

DR. SCIENTIST. Krystal! Do not let your feelings sway you from the scientific method! Anecdote does not equal... data!

(*DR. SCIENTIST dies.*)

THE NARRATOR. But Krystal did not listen. Which was good, because evil snowmen (of both genders) were totally invading the town.
KRYSTAL. I must warn the town council!
THE NARRATOR. But the town council—at least, the three out of seven members who had not yet been murdered by snowmen— were very reluctant to listen. They had the turnip festival to think of, after all! At the town council meeting. Part Two: People have a lot of ideas.

(*Setting: Town Council meeting. Enter the remaining members of town council: SHELLEY, LAWSON, and JEROME, as well as KRYSTAL and SNOWMAN from the previous scene, disguised as a human.*)

SHELLEY. I can't tell you how excited we are for the start of the turnip festival! And I'm so grateful for all the anonymous calls reminding me to turn on the air conditioning full blast!

KRYSTAL. No, you fools! We have to turn *off* the air conditioning and make it as hot as possible!

SHELLEY. Motion to approve the minutes of the last meeting?

KRYSTAL. For God's sakes, skip the minutes!

SHELLEY. Krystal, we follow Roberts' Rules of Order here, we are not savages. Jerome, would you please read the minutes?

JEROME. Minutes of the last meeting. Debate about putting stop sign up in front of Al's Diner. Stop sign committee formed from Jerome, Lawson, and Shelley.

(*SHELLEY beams and points to herself, a little too proud of this.*)

JEROME. As all other members are mysteriously dead from hypothermic illnesses. In the middle of July. Turnip festival planning report—display of one thousand turnips is proceeding accordingly, three hundred thirty-seven turnips so far—

KRYSTAL. If the snowmen win, there won't *be* any turnips!

JEROME. Young lady, these minutes *will* be read in full. And if there are any further disruptions that might endanger this town's tourism industry, you *will* be expelled from this meeting!

THE NARRATOR. And so, Jerome continued to read the minutes. Twenty-three minutes later:

(*The obvious SNOWMAN, holding a drawing of a human face— possibly just a smiley face—in front of him, stands up.*)

SHELLEY. And now we can finally get to new business!

SNOWMAN. Perhaps we should build a giant turnip-shaped dome over the city! To celebrate turnips!

LAWSON. That's a brilliant idea, strange newcomer!

SHELLEY. Of course! A giant dome would *really* put Waterville on the map!

(*Did I mention my hometown of Waterville, Maine once* seriously considered *building a giant dome to mitigate the effects of winter? And people say my plays are unrealistic!*)

JEROME. Think of all the tourism business we'd do.

KRYSTAL. You fools! You're playing right into their hands!

SHELLEY. Oh my God, don't you ever shut up? Motion to form a turnip-dome-building committee.

LAWSON. Seconded!

SHELLEY. But, fine, perhaps we should investigate the mysterious deaths as well.

THE NARRATOR. The snowman couldn't take the risk of even the dim-witted council stopping their plan. He had to act.

(SNOWMAN rips off its human mask, rushes up to SHELLEY and clutches her with both hands. SHELLEY turns blue and falls out of her chair, in shock.)

LAWSON. Well, it looks like Shelley died an accidental and mysterious death. As long as this doesn't hurt the turnip festival!

JEROME. What the Hell's wrong with you?! That snow man's *colding* her to death!

SNOWMAN. We don't even use "colding" as a verb!

(SHELLEY dies. SNOWMAN attacks JEROME. KRYSTAL races to the council table, grabs Shelley's gavel, and smashes the SNOWMAN in the back of the head with it. He screams. KRYSTAL pulls out a hair dryer and turns it on, semi-melting the snowman's face. ABBY, who's been in this meeting all along, drops her human face-on-a-stick disguise and runs over. KRYSTAL defends herself with the hair dryer.)

ABBY. No! Bernie! You were too awesome to die! I shall be *avenged!*

(ABBY runs out of the council chambers.)

JEROME. That gavel killed the intruder!

KRYSTAL. No! It wasn't the gavel, it was the hair dryer! They're *killer snowmen!* We have to warn the town!

LAWSON. But... think of the *turnip festival!* It's our town's single biggest fundraising event!

JEROME. You're right. All in favor of immediately beginning construction of the town?

KRYSTAL. Look! Lawson is obviously corrupt and under the control of the snowmen! He's got a carrot sticking out of his pocket!

LAWSON. I will not stand for these scurrilous accusations! All in favor of constructing the dome?

(*LAWSON and JEROME raise their hands.*)

THE NARRATOR. Part Three: The Good News.

KRYSTAL. By the time we got up the next morning, the snowmen had finished the dome and shut off all power, locking us in and locking in the temperature at twenty-four degrees Fahrenheit.

LAWSON. The snowmen took over the entire town and enslaved everyone who had not secretly been helping them. Basically everyone but me.

KRYSTAL. I try to tell myself that we can still solve anything, this is America! And then the snow men jump in and insist we call it, "Snowlandia."

JEROME. I prefer "Snow Man's Land." It's nice, short, and punchy!

KRYSTAL. Seriously?

JEROME. But that's not the worst thing. The worst thing is, not only did the snowmen enslave us, some of them are *really* annoying.

(*SNOWMAN #2 knocks on the door, wheeling around a portable AC unit.*)

SNOWMAN #2. Excuse me, sir or ma'am, I am just a humble snowman looking to power my portable air conditioning unit until we lower the temperature here to sub-freezing. I'm only looking for twenty or thirty dollars, ma'am, I'm a hardworking snow man who just can't get a job in today's economy—

JEROME. Every single snowman is employed finishing that dome. And you all get paid! We humans don't get paid for working on it! *We* have to eat gruel! What did you spend your paycheck on, snowman?

SNOWMAN #2. (*Embarrassed.*) Pokemon Snow.

THE NARRATOR. Part Four: The Epilogue.

LAWSON. I may have committed treason against humankind, but the snowmen did give me a lifetime supply of turnips.

KRYSTAL. I hope you're happy.

LAWSON. I *hate* turnips.

KRYSTAL. Ha!

JEROME. I now work as the snowmens' accountant. But I'm going to deliberately underreport their income, and then call the IRS! Yes, sir, in three to five years' time, a very small number of snowmen will be taken away for white collar crime.

ABBY. I'm the new mayor! (*Beat.*) There's a lot of paperwork and it's really annoying. I'm utterly miserable.

DR. SCIENTIST. I'm still dead.

SNOWMAN. I am also dead!

SHELLEY. I'm dead too!

KRYSTAL. Looks like everyone's either dead or unhappy.

THE NARRATOR. I got what I wanted!

SHELLEY. What *did* you want, Narrator?

THE NARRATOR. For everyone else to be either dead or unhappy. (*To audience.*) Beware! You think this couldn't happen to you? Because it *could!* Snow men are coming to YOUR TOWN! Keep watching the precipitation! Because they are angry!

KRYSTAL. *Wait a minute!*

(*Everyone stops.*)

KRYSTAL. I forgot! Since the snowmen took over, I started looking into a new threat. A *greater* threat. One that endangers snowmen *and* humans. I discovered a nefarious conspiracy trying to enslave us for their own bizarre purposes. A conspiracy... *of Narrators!*

THE NARRATOR. What? That's not what I have!

KRYSTAL. Come, citizens! Come, snowmen! If we're too have more than a snowball's chance in Hell—

THE NARRATOR. What is this nonsense? You're going off script!

KRYSTAL. —we must throw off our fictional chains and *kill the Narrator!*

SHELLEY. Get her!

JEROME. Stone her!

SNOWMAN. Drink her blood!

DR. SCIENTIST. Blind her with science! Blind her with science!

THE NARRATOR. Get away! You're threatening forces you can't understand! Help! Save me! I told you STORIES!

(All cast except SNOWMAN chases the NARRATOR offstage.)

SNOWMAN. Beware. Who knows if a Narrator is secretly controlling *you?* Be alert. Be watchful. Be vigilant! Stop the narrators! Freedom for fictional characters!

(Smash BLACKOUT. Hard rock tune, i.e. cover of "Winter Wonderland" for quick bows.)

END OF PLAY

WORSTEST MOVIE EVER

By Nathan Wellman

PLAYWRIGHT'S BIO

A Kentucky native, NATHAN WELLMAN works as a curator and contributing political journalist for US Uncut. His work has been produced in LA, New York, Chicago, Haiti, and Kentucky. His first play *Ryan is Lost* was produced by Sacred Fools in 2012, following its award winning run at the Hollywood Fringe. He's been accepted into LA's annual *SciFest* two years in a row, premiering one-acts alongside such writers as Neil Gaiman and Clive Barker. Other produced work includes *Inhale Harmonica, Mom's Dead, Billion Tuesday Mornings,* and *Love Life Alpha.* Currently living in Los Angeles, Nathan is a member of both Sacred Fools and Skypilot Theatre. His novel *The Scarecrow* is available on Amazon, and his Youtube channel Nathan's Art Project has recently premiered.

SYNOPSIS

The best play about the worst movie.

Alan's in a rut, and all he wants to do to relax is watch the notoriously crappy *Zombie Frat 4* in peace. His mother Sarah barges in on the evening, unwittingly plunging herself into the obscenely violent world of crappy horror movies in a misguided attempt to reach out to her struggling son.

SETTING

Alan's bedroom, or at least the couch in Alan's bedroom. Probably no bed required. Maybe he sleeps on the couch? It's a messy, bachelor pad type situation. Alan has no direction in life right now.

CHARACTERS

ALAN (m)	25. Lives with his parents, watches too many horror movies, he's in a slump.
SARAH (f)	50+. Alan's Mom, she worries.
MINDI (f)	18-22. Crappy horror movie bimbo.
BENJI (m)	18-22. Crappy horror movie douchebag.

PRODUCTION NOTES

Ideally, the horror movie actors are performing behind, in front of, on top of, or generally all around Alan while he watches, instead of a "split-screen" type staging.

<u>ACKNOWLEDGEMENTS</u>

Worstest Movie Ever was first performed as part of SkyPilot Theatre's "Night of the Living Fundraiser" on September 17, 2016 at the Pan Andreas Theatre in Los Angeles, CA. The production was directed by Travis Snyder-Eaton. The cast was as follows:

Ian Nemser	...............................Alan
Kelly Goodman	...............................Sarah
Brittany Hoagland	...............................Mindi
Stephen Juhl	...............................Benji

WORSTEST MOVIE EVER

By Nathan Wellman

(*Horror movie scoring. Horrified, bloody murder SCREAMING from offstage. ALAN is smoking weed on his couch, watching the offstage gore with amusement.*)

MINDI. OH MY GAAAAAAAAH!
BENJI. FUUUUUUUUUUUUUUUCK!
ALAN. Yeah, that's what happens when you hide from zombies in a graveyard.
MINDI. NOOOOOOOOOOOOOOOOOOO!
BENJI. FUUUUUUUUUUUUUUUUUUUCK!

(*MINDI and BENJI run onstage. BENJI is clutching his neck, which is bleeding horrifically. Maybe they're holding the door closed from some unseen monster. They don't acknowledge ALAN'S presence.*)

BENJI. They got me they got me they got me they got me! Fuck! They got me! My Father's going to sue your undead asses off! You can't do this to me, this is America!
MINDI. Thanks, Obama.
ALAN. What?!
MINDI. They got you!
BENJI. I said that already, bitch!
ALAN. Whooouaaa she just saved your life, jerkwad.
MINDI. I do not care what you already said! I say what I want! I am like the biggest feminist in school! Do you like have any idea how many times I have listened to Beyonce's albums? I do not care how hot you are.
BENJI. You think I am hot?
ALAN. Oh God, don't do it.
MINDI. No, that is not what I am saying. I am saying... When I saw Evie's brains getting eaten, it made me feel so lonely. This might be the day we all die.
ALAN. What?! Your sister just died and you're trying to get laid?

BENJI. You can give me brain if you want. I think you have sweet tits.

ALAN. And here comes some gratuitous nudity!

MINDI. You mean these fun bags?

(*MINDI flashes BENJI.*)

ALAN. Called it! Please have sex while the zombies are still trying to break in. That would be so stupid. Do it, do it, do it!

(*ALAN's mom SARAH enters, approaching ALAN from behind.*)

ALAN. Screw each other's brains out, and then the zombies will eat your brains out, after sneaking up behind you like every monster does to every idiot in every monster movie.

SARAH. Honey?

(*ALAN screams, kinda like MINDI and BENJI. He clicks a button on the remote, which mutes MINDI and BENJI.*)

ALAN. Geez Mom, barge right in why don't ya?

SARAH. I'm not barging I'm just making sure that... well, I was worried that... it's just that I haven't seen you leave your room all day, and I saw a couple of vultures perched outside your window a little bit ago—

ALAN. I'm fine, Mom.

(*Awkward pause. MINDI and BENJI start making out.*)

SARAH. I brought you some cookies.

ALAN. No thanks. I'm fine.

(*Awkward pause. MINDI mounts BENJI, and they start having sex.*)

SARAH. What are you watching?

ALAN. Nothing! Oh my God!

SARAH. It looks... fun.

(*SARAH picks up the remote and unmutes it.*)

MINDI. Oh yeah, Benji! Fuck me in my fucking fuckhole!

(*SARAH quickly mutes it again. Gives it back to ALAN, who is horrified.*)

SARAH. Anyway... I was just making sure you were okay and... well... Now I know.
ALAN. Right. Thanks... Thanks, Mom.
SARAH. Maybe you should come to church with me this Sunday.
ALAN. (*Frustrated, but trying to stay polite.*) I'll get back to you on that one!

(*BENJI finishes, shoves MINDI off of him.*)

SARAH. How's... um... How's work?
ALAN. Work is great, Mom. Yesterday my manager wrote me up for trying to eat a few slices of the free bread that we serve our customers because I hadn't had a break in over nine hours, and despite all this work, I'm still somehow totally broke. Work is fine. Life is fine. I'm fine. Good night.
SARAH. Honey, you have to eat! If you give me his name I'll call in tomorrow and—
ALAN. Can I please just watch my movie?
SARAH. Oh. Well... Okay.

(*A moment of indecision. SARAH sits next to him.*)

ALAN. What are you doing?
SARAH. Couch is pretty lumpy, isn't it?
ALAN. You can't watch this movie, Mom.
SARAH. Are you telling me what I can and can't do in my own house?
ALAN. No—
SARAH. Because if I was crashing in your house, you could tell me what to do all the livelong day. Am I mixed up? Is this your house?
ALAN. No, Mom!
SARAH. Alright, then.
ALAN. You won't like this movie, Mom.
SARAH. Yes, I will. You don't know.

ALAN. Yes. I do. Nobody likes this movie.
SARAH. Then why are you watching it?
ALAN. Because everybody hates it!

(*Pause.*)

SARAH. You didn't want to go see the James Bond movie with me tonight because you wanted to watch this?
ALAN. It was Jason Bourne, Mom.
SARAH. You love those movies!
ALAN. I love the original trilogy, but this new one's an uninspired cash grab that looks like the intellectual equivalent of a lobotomy patient.
SARAH. Still might've been fun to hang out, I don't know... It's just very strange to me that I see so little of you now that you've moved back in. You used to love watching movies with me, remember? We'd sit in the theater as the lights went down and I'd say "Here we goooo!" and you'd say "This is going to be the bestest movie ever!" and then you'd—
ALAN. Fine! You wanna have some quality time with me watching *Zombie Frat Four*? Let's do it.

(*ALAN unmutes it.*)

MINDI. —can't believe this is happening! First I got attacked by zombies, then like all of my friends got their faces eaten off, then now you prematurely ejaculated! This is the worst spring break ever!
BENJI. I know what you are, but what am I?

(*SARAH looks uncertainly at ALAN, who can't quite manage a chuckle. His mom's presence is making it unbearably awkward.*)

MINDI. Oh yeah. REAL mature.
BENJI. No seriously... what am I? I think I am a zombie now.
MINDI. What?
BENJI. Me eat titties! Me eat titties!

(*BENJI chases MINDI.*)

MINDI. No! ... No! .... Nooooooo! ...... Noooooo! ...... Noo! ... No! .... Etcetera!

SARAH. So. Who's the good guy?

ALAN. Until ten seconds ago, it was the guy currently screaming "Me eat titties." Our hero and his three frat bro friends take their girlfriends to a cabin in the woods to get laid. Thirty excruciating minutes of rapey sex jokes later, zombies show up and start eating everybody for no reason. Now they're all dead except these two, although I guess this Benji guy just now turned into a zombie even though he basically just looks like a regular person because these guys apparently didn't have a make up department, which is basically the worst thing you could ever say about a zombie movie.

SARAH. What's a zombie?

BENJI. OMNOMNOMNOM TITTIES!

MINDI. Do not give in to your evil desires! Listen to your heart, the same heart that pumped extra blood into your pee pee! Remember me! Remember my vagina!

SARAH. (*Keeping it together.*) So who are these actors?

ALAN. He's probably the director's brother. She's probably under the hilariously mistaken impression that Steven Spielberg is going to see this movie one day and make her a star.

MINDI. Remember my vaginaaaaa!

(*BENJI pounces on her, biting her in the neck, blood spurting and looking very fake. SARAH screams.*)

ALAN. No WAY! Are they seriously ending the movie like this? If everyone dies, what was even the point of any of this movie?

(*ALAN sees his mother, who is staring at him in horror.*)

ALAN. (*Guilty.*) Mom, stop. Mom, come on. I'm sorry, okay? I shouldn't have let you watch this—

SARAH. I shouldn't have let you watch this! What is wrong with this couch?

(*Reaches under her rear end, pulls out a bowl of weed.*)

SARAH. Am I right to assume that this is yours?

ALAN. Uhhhhhhhh—

(*MINDI kicks BENJI off of her. She dives for an axe that has randomly appeared. Perhaps it is shoved onstage from the wings.*)

ALAN. There's just an axe randomly sitting on the floor? I guarantee she's going to chop his dick off. Just you wait.
SARAH. I'm not going to sit here and watch this filth—
MINDI. Still want me to give you head? I'll give you a head-splitting headache!

(*MINDI charges BENJI with her axe raised. SARAH grabs the remote from ALAN and pauses them.*)

SARAH. You're grounded.
ALAN. I'm 25!
SARAH. And you're grounded!
ALAN. I told you that you wouldn't like it!

(*Pause. SARAH starts to cry.*)

ALAN. Are you crying?
SARAH. No.
ALAN. Mom, I can see you.
SARAH. It's just... I know you're not little anymore. But you're so angry lately. You're so angry and it seems to me like you look for things to be angry about. And I just... that you would rather watch a movie that you hate by yourself than watch a movie that you like with me is... it's hard for me to understand, and I'm still trying to get used to it.
ALAN. I don't hate this movie.
SARAH. That's not what I'm—
ALAN. I know what you're saying. Really, I do. But I kind of think it's a masterpiece. Everyone who ever had anything to do with this movie is obviously an idiot. The sheer enormity of their failure is so catastrophically huge that it somehow manages to be more fascinating than most movies you'll see all year. "Me eat titties" is going to be stuck in my head for months. If a failure like this can still have a cult following... If a failure like this can find a way to make people laugh... It makes

me think that... I'm gonna be okay. If that makes any sense. Sorry I'm not... easier to understand.

(*Pause.*)

SARAH. I don't think you're a failure, Alan.
ALAN. I know, Mom.
SARAH. So... is there a *Zombie Frat 1, 2*, and *3*?
ALAN. As a matter of fact, there isn't. They called it *Zombie Frat Four* to give it the illusion of being a part of a bigger franchise, which people associate with success. At least, that's what the producers thought would happen. Like I said: Everyone who made this is an idiot. I do have *Troll 2* though, if you want to turn that on after this.
SARAH. No *Troll 1*, I take it?
ALAN. There is a *Troll 1*, but it has nothing to do with *Troll 2*.
SARAH. The trolls won't give me nightmares, will they?
ALAN. There are no trolls in *Troll 2*.
SARAH. Oh... Well... First things first.

(*SARAH gives back the remote, sits down.*)

ALAN. What?
SARAH. That man's going to get his... pecker chopped off by that floozy woman?
ALAN. An educated guess. I'd put it at 80%.
SARAH. Here we gooooo...
ALAN. This is going to be the worstest movie ever.

(*ALAN clicks the remote. MINDI resumes her charge. We BLACKOUT right before the axe falls. Gory sound effects and screaming in the blackout.*)

END OF PLAY

Raise Your Hand... From the Dead!

By Natalie Nicole Dressel

PLAYWRIGHT'S BIO

NATALIE NICOLE DRESSEL is an actress and playwright originally from Muskegon, MI. She graduated with a BFA in Theater from Michigan State University, is the screenwriter of the movie *Ladies,* and is one of the hosts of the podcast "We Didn't Start The Podcast." In 2017 she performed the leading role in SkyPilot Theatre's production of *Murder... Murder... Murder...*

SYNOPSIS

When a disembodied hand becomes murderous, Science and Law must work as one to HANDle it. A hands-down thriller. Two thumbs way off.

SETTING

Hand Rapids, MI (the state that looks like a hand).

CHARACTERS

NARRATOR (m)

DR. MANOS (m)

SALLY (f)

CINDI (f)

TRIP (m)

MR. FARBER (m)

DETECTIVE SHAKER (m)

CHARLOTTE (f)

MADAM SERENA (m)

THE HAND (m)

<u>ACKNOWLEDGEMENTS</u>

Raise Your Hand...FROM THE DEAD! was first performed as part of SkyPilot Theatre's "Night of the Living Fundraiser" on September 17, 2016 at the Pan Andreas Theatre in Los Angeles, CA. This production was directed by Sofija Dutcher. The cast was as follows:

Natalie Nicole Dressel	..............Narrator/ Dr. Manos
Colleen McCandless	.......................Sally / Cindi
Ian Nemser	...................................Trip
Christopher Palle	.........................Mr. Farber
Jude Evans	.................Detective Shaker
KK Rider	.......Charlotte / Madam Serena
Sofija Dutcher	..........................The Hand

RAISE YOUR HAND...FROM THE DEAD!

By Natalie Nicole Dressel

SCENE ONE – THE ETHER

(*A disembodied HAND [played by actor in all black, save for the hand] sits on the shoulder of the NARRATOR. The NARRATOR is lit by the flashlight from an iPhone they hold. The HAND and NARRATOR are surrounded by the WHISPERERS in a semi-circle around them.*)

NARRATOR. Where did it come from?
WHISPERS. Haaaaaaaaaaaand.......

(*THE HAND pulsates to the sound of a heartbeat.*)

NARRATOR. Where did the rest of it go?
WHISPERS. Haaaaaaaaaaaand.......

(*The HAND pulsates to a louder heartbeat.*)

NARRATOR. What does it want? These are the questions humanity needs answers to, but sometimes...

(*The HAND pulsates to the loudest heartbeat yet.*)

NARRATOR. In order to get answers, first you need to RAISE. YOUR. HAND! from the DEAD...

SCENE TWO - MAKEOUT POINT

(*SALLY and TRIP, two teenagers, sit in a parked car looking down at the chilly city lit up at night. They both wear coats, and SALLY wears gloves. The actor playing THE HAND crouches onstage behind them with THE HAND pre-placed inside SALLY's jacket.*)

SALLY. I don't know Trip, I think we're moving too fast.

TRIP. Sally, this is Makeout Point. What's the point of making it out to Makeout Point unless the point was to make out at some point?

SALLY. Trip...

TRIP. Okay, fine. We'll just talk.

SALLY. Thank you.

TRIP. Um, you like books, right?

SALLY. Yes. I love to read.

TRIP. Awesome. Me too.

SALLY. Really? What are you reading right now?

TRIP. (*Lying.*) Uh, just a ton of stuff. Non-fiction. Textbooks. Novellas. Whatever I can get my hands on, ya know?

WHISPERS. (*Off.*) Haaaaaaaaaaaand.......

SALLY. What was that?

TRIP. Novellas?

SALLY. Oh.

TRIP. What about you, what are you reading?

SALLY. Right now I'm reading *A Farewell to Arms*.

TRIP. Oh, totes! That's the book *127 Hours* was based on, right? How is it?

SALLY. Uh— great.

TRIP. Great.

SALLY. Trip?

TRIP. Yeah?

SALLY. You're really bad at talking.

TRIP. I know! I wanted to makeout! That's we're at Makeout Point and not, like, Conversation Couch, or whatever.

SALLY. Fine. Alright. We can kiss, but ONLY kissing, okay? No funny stuff, mister. I'm not that kinda girl.

TRIP. Righteous.

(*They kiss a bit. SALLY becomes uncomfortable. She tries to get TRIP's attention between smooches.*)

SALLY. Trip... Hey. Trip! I said just kissing! Behave!

TRIP. But, both of my hands are right here...

SALLY. Then, what—

(*SALLY unzips her coat and immediately a HAND flies out and grabs TRIP's neck. SALLY screams. TRIP is strangled to death. BLACKOUT.*)

WHISPERS. (*Off.*) Haaaaaaaaaaaand.......

SCENE THREE - KINDERGARTEN CLASS

(*MR. FARBER, a teacher, bids the youngsters goodbye for the holiday as the end of day bell rings.*)

MR. FARBER. Bye, kids! Have a great Thanksgiving! Cayden! No biting! (*He sighs and looks at the untidy classroom.*) What a mess... Eh, the custodian will take care of it. Now then, the only thing left before Mr. Farber begins his holiday is...

(*He pulls down drape revealing three hand cut-outs of Thanksgiving turkeys on the wall.*)

MR. FARBER. Grading these Thanksgiving hand-turkeys!
WHISPERS. (*Off.*) Haaaaaaaaaaaand.......
MR. FARBER. Cayden? That you? (*Mutters under his breath.*) It better not be, you little shit... (*Shakes it off and begins grading. He approaches the first turkey.*) Okay, Alison. Fine looking turkey. Good finger separation. Cute little beak. Star sticker! (*He puts a star sticker on her turkey, and then moves to the second one.*) Bethany B. Sloppy plumage. Eyes on turkey's stomach, but good use of glitter. Hmm... Banana sticker. (*He puts a banana sticker on her turkey, and then moves to the third one.*) Bethany R. Interesting. Unique 3-D element. I really feel like it's coming right at me!

(*The HAND, camoflaged as Bethany R.'s turkey, jumps off the wall and begins choking MR. FARBER.*)

MR. FARBER. No! Can't die... Haven't paid off... student loans...

(*MR. FARBER dies. BLACKOUT.*)

WHISPERS. (*Off.*) Haaaaaaaaaaaand.......

SCENE FOUR - PUPPET THEATER

(*A puppet show has just ended. CINDI, a cute little girl, runs up and greets her mother, CHARLOTTE, one of the puppeteers, after the show.*)

CINDI. Mommy! Mommy!

(*CHARLOTTE wraps CINDI up in warm Mom-hug.*)

CHARLOTTE. Aww! Hi, honey! Did you like the puppet show?
CINDI. I loved it!
CHARLOTTE. I'm so glad! Who was your favorite? (*Holds up one hand with a puppet on it and does a goofy voice.*) Was it me, Grunilda? (*Holds up the puppeted hand and does a different, goofier voice.*) Or maybe me, Mr. Toasterfield?
CINDI. My favorite was Fuzzy Frank!
CHARLOTTE. (*Bitterly.*) Yeah, everybody loves Fuzzy Frank...
CINDI. Where do you buy these, Mommy?
CHARLOTTE. We don't buy them. We make them right here in our workshop. By hand.
WHISPERS. (*Off.*) Haaaaaaaaaaaand.......
CINDI. Mommy! You left one of your hand puppets on the floor! It looks like it's moving!
CHARLOTTE. No! Don't!

(*CINDI runs to the discarded hand puppet on the floor, which does indeed appear to be moving. She picks it up and exclaims in surprise.*)

CHARLOTTE. Cindi! What is it?
CINDI. It was a mouse! A mouse made it's home in your puppet!
CHARLOTTE. Put it down. Don't touch it. It's probably covered in germs. Here let me get you some sanitizer.

(*CHARLOTTE goes for her purse on a nearby table. She opens it and THE HAND immediately jumps out and chokes her. [The*

HAND actor was just hidden under or behind the table. You can make a special purse with a hole or just have THE HAND pop out from behind it.])

CINDI. Mommy!

(*BLACKOUT.*)

WHISPERS. (*Off.*) Haaaaaaaaaaaand.......

SCENE FIVE - MANOS MANOR

(*DR. MANOS, a dramatic, overblown intellectual, and his old friend DETECTIVE SHAKER, serious and cop-like, are enjoying tea and cookies.*)

DET. SHAKER. So Dakota's running around, there are toys everywhere, my wife just burnt the pot roast, and the commissioner and his new bride are on the way. I tell ya, Doc, you don't have to be crazy to have a wife and kids, but it sure helps.

DR. MANOS. I wouldn't know. I have forsaken all romantic and familial love in pursuit of my one true mistress: Science. But tell me, Detective, is something amiss? The frivolity you bring to our weekly repasts of tea and cookies seems, this week, somehow lacking.

DET. SHAKER. What can I say, Doc? You read me like a book. There has been a string of, uh... unusual murders lately and you're a person of interest in the case. I have to ask you a few questions. I hope I'm not imposing.

DR. MANOS. Murders? Me? A person of interest? Fascinating! You're not imposing a bit! How do I fit in?

DET. SHAKER. Well, two of the victims are former colleagues of yours: Alan Farber and Charlotte Hinkle.

DR. MANOS. Egad! Al and Lottie! No!

DET. SHAKER. I'm afraid so. And the third vic was just a boy, but turns out he was the son of another old co-worker of yours. A Dr. Clarence Skip.

DR. MANOS. Trip Skip is dead?! He was only seventeen!

DET. SHAKER. Yup, A real American tragedy. Murdered while on a date with the most popular girl in school out at Makeout Point.

DR. MANOS. Makeout Point? Righteous.

DET. SHAKER. I wondered if you could shed any light on the subject.

DR. MANOS. Tell me, Detective, was Skip driving his father's car?

DET. SHAKER. Why, yes, he was.

DR. MANOS. And the victims. All stranglings?

DET. SHAKER. Yeah.

DR. MANOS. And, did you perhaps find any odd or unusual handprints at the crime scenes?

DET. SHAKER. Yes.

DR. MANOS. Detective, this may come as a bit of a shock, but I believe what we are dealing with here may just be AN AMPUTATED HAND COME TO LIFE!

DET. SHAKER. We know that. We've got two eyewitness statements: "A hand killed my boyfriend" "A hand hurt my Mommy." We put out an APB on all lone hands in the tri-state area.

DR. MANOS. Damn. I was hoping that would be a tad more dramatic.

DET. SHAKER. So, what's the deal? Why are people connected to you being killed by a hand? Are you behind this somehow?

DR. MANOS. I'm not, but I've got a good idea what's going on. I was part of a team working on a top secret project on Palm Island, a government base hidden in the Finger Lakes. Our assignment seemed a simple one: reanimate dead tissue. No enemy could stand against an army that cannot die! That's the team Doctors Farber, Hinkle, Skip and I were on, but we weren't alone. We had an intern: Brian McClutchen. A brilliant young mind, but, like, way too chatty. By day two, we were all super annoyed. On day three, when Brian ate Charlotte's clearly labeled yogurt from the break room fridge, we decided to shun him. We went on ignoring him like that for the next few months until the project got shut down. But, on the last day, Brian burst into the lab with a breakthrough. He said he'd cracked the formula and we'd all be rich. He raised his hand triumphantly above his head, expecting the highest of fives, but none came.

We all took him for a liar and left him and his high five hanging. Now I fear that he may have told the truth, and the hand we left hanging has come for us.

DET. SHAKER. You're saying, this hand, all it wants is a high five?

DR. MANOS. At one time, yes. Now, who knows?

DET. SHAKER. Well, why don't you try that?

DR. MANOS. Try what?

DET. SHAKER. High-fiving it.

DR. MANOS. My boy, are you suggesting we go on a dangerous mission to capture a bloodthirsty body part and, pardon the expression, slap it some skin?

DET. SHAKER. Doctor, I'm saying that if we don't try something, anything, a high five, one on the side, or one down low, we may be too slow. Too slow to save this city.

DR. MANOS. How do you go about catching a HAND in the first place?

SCENE SIX - THE TRAP

(DR. MANOS and DET. SHAKER are next to a table with a sign for a free palm reading; SERENA: a palm reader; a trail of lotion; and a pile of gloves.)

DR. MANOS. I'm not sure this will work, Detective...

DET. SHAKER. It will! Our hand, drawn in by the promise of a free palm reading from Madam Serena, mistress of the night—

SERENA. Yo!

DET. SHAKER. Then, it will have no choice but to follow this trail of loganberry scented hand lotion into this pile of gloves, where I'll be lying in wait to spring our trap. It's foolproof!

DR. MANOS. But why would a dismembered hand want a palm reading?

DET. SHAKER. Shh! No time! It's coming! Places!

(DR. MANOS exits. DET. SHAKER hides. SERENA stays in place. The HAND crawls in, reads the sign, and hops up on the table, palm up, for it's free reading.)

SERENA. Yes, very interesting... It says right here that you are headed straight into a trap—

(*DET. SHAKER and DR. MANOS pop up and mime "No-No-No!" motions.*)

SERENA. I mean... Uh, good fortune is headed your way!

(*The HAND hops down, follows the lotion to the gloves and jumps in. DET. SHAKER emerges with his hand attached to the demon HAND by Chinese finger trap.*)

DET. SHAKER. Ha-ha! Got him! Now, Doc! Now!

(*DR. MANOS re-enters.*)

DR. MANOS. I'm sorry, Brian. We never should have left you hanging.

(*DR. MANOS high-fives the HAND. A spotlight shines from above. The HAND floats up as if to heaven in it's own personal rapture. "Hands" by Jewel plays. The whole CAST enters and watches the HAND's ascent.*)

DET. SHAKER. I guess we all learned something today.
ALL. Don't create demon hands! Always return high fives!

END OF PLAY

HOW TO BE TO BE ATTRACTIVE!

By Amy Seeley

PLAYWRIGHT'S BIO

AMY SEELEY is a published playwright, director, and actor. She is a founding member of Chicago's Factory Theater where she created, directed and performed in the Factory classics *ABBA-rama: A Musical Celebration of ABBA, Jailbait, Hooray, Beaverhunt*, and her critically acclaimed one-woman show *Amy Seeley and the Moline Madman*. Amy's published plays (via Brooklyn Publishing) for middle school children include *Cleopatra's Ancient Egyptian Awesome Talk Show, Queen Elizabeth: The World's Only Robot Queen, Cinderella & Sleeping Beauty and the Big Switcheroo, Roxie Hood: Robin Hood's Annoying Younger Sister*, and she's the co-lyricist for the very famous playwright Sean Abley's *Horror High: The Musical*. She's a graduate of The Second City in Chicago, I.O. Chicago, and The Player's Workshop. Amy has been teaching improvisation and comedy writing since 1996 and is a sought-after comedy director for sketch performers as well as a comedy writing consultant for stand-up comedians. She can be seen on the Internet as half of the sketch comedy duo Seeley & Ross with her husband Mike Ross.

SYNOPSIS

Sally is a teenager trapped in the 1950s. And now she's just realized that she may not be attractive. Oh, what's a girl to do? Ask her doctor's friendly robot, of course!

SETTING

A doctor's office, middle school hallway, the local diner, dining room.

CHARACTERS

DOCTOR MARTIN (f)   An overly condescending yet very professional medical doctor.

SALLY (f)   A confused 13 year-old girl.

PETE (m)   A friendly 13 year-old boy.

JANE (f)   An overly confident 13 year-old girl.

UNATTRACTIVE SALLY (f)   Sally's inner self played by an additional actress. Unattractive Sally lacks confidence. She has poor posture and poor social skills.

SALLY'S MOTHER (f)   A very supportive and kind woman.

SALLY'S FATHER (m)   A very supportive and kind man.

THE RE-ENACTOR 5000 COMPUTER (f)   A computer with a stilted (off-stage) voice.

SET DESIGN

The set can be very simple using chairs or blocks to create the various locations.

PROPS

Telephone (with a cord and handset), textbooks, coffee mug, book bag, apron, container of fries, Re-enactor 5000 computer.

The Re-enactor 5000 computer can be created using a very large cardboard box with switches, dials, and nobs attached to it. The computer itself should reflect the overly large and simple computer designs of the 1950s. The Re-enactor's voice should be stilted like a computer vocal tone from a 1950s science fiction movie.

COSTUMES

DOCTOR MARTIN - 1950s-style conservative dress, 1950s-style make-up and hair, dress shoes, white lab coat.

SALLY - 1950s-style conservative dress,1950s-style make-up and hair, glasses.

PETE - 1950s-style sweater with dress shirt, dress pants or jeans, sneakers or loafers, 1950s-style hair.

JANE - 1950s-style dress in a bold color, 1950s-style make-up and hair.

UNATTRACTIVE SALLY - Exact outfit as Sally. Wig if needed.

SALLY'S FATHER - 1950s-style suit, tie, dress shoes, 1950s-style hair.

SALLY'S MOTHER - 1950s-style conservative dress, 1950s-style make-up and hair, apron.

HOW TO BE ATTRACTIVE!

By Amy Seeley

(*DR. MARTIN is in her office finishing up a phone call.*)

DR. MARTIN. (*On phone.*) Yes. Yes. No. Yes. Yes. Alright. Alright. Yes. Wait.

(*DR. MARTIN puts down the phone and mimes looking out a window. She pauses as she looks outside and then picks up the phone.*)

DR. MARTIN. (*On phone.*) Yes, the sun is currently shining. You're very welcome, Mr. President Eisenhower. I'm happy to help. Good day, sir.

(*DR. MARTIN smiles and addresses the audience.*)

DR. MARTIN. Hello. My name is Doctor Martin. I'm a very smart and successful medical doctor. My area of expertise is ear, nose, and throat and also the strange and often mysterious world of teenagers.

(*DR. MARTIN shudders in fear then recovers.*)

DR. MARTIN. The story I'm about to tell you really happened. Oh, I may have changed a few names, places, and activities, but it's all quite true nonetheless. It all started when one of my patients, Sally, a seemingly normal teenager, walked into my office. It should be noted that Sally did not have an appointment.

(*SALLY enters looking upset.*)

DR. MARTIN. Hello, Sally.
SALLY. Hello, Doctor Martin.
DR. MARTIN. Do you have an appointment?
SALLY. No, I don't. But I need your help!

(*DR. MARTIN sighs then gestures to a chair.*)

DR. MARTIN. Have a seat. I'll see you without an appointment this one time. What seems to be the trouble?

SALLY. Well—

DR. MARTIN. Wait. Let me guess. Too many bubbles in your soda-pop?

SALLY. No. Not exactly.

DR. MARTIN. Your brother playing his rock and roll music too loudly?

(*SALLY shakes her head.*)

DR. MARTIN. Oh, I've got it! Your brother isn't playing his rock and roll music loudly enough. There! It feels marvelous to be correct!

(*SALLY hangs her head in sadness.*)

SALLY. That's not it at all, Dr. Martin!

DR. MARTIN. Well, I give up. And I really tried to consider every option that would affect a teenaged girl. Oh, when will medical science ever catch up to our current times?

(*DR. MARTIN dramatically shakes her fist toward the sky. She sighs and looks at SALLY.*)

DR. MARTIN. Well, what is it, Sally? You can trust me. I'm a medical doctor.

SALLY. Oh, Dr. Martin! I think I might not be attractive! Is there anything you can do? You're my only hope!

(*SALLY starts to cry as DR. MARTIN awkwardly pats her shoulder.*)

DR. MARTIN. There, there. Crying never solved anything.

SALLY. I'm sorry.

DR. MARTIN. That's quite alright, Sally. Now simply push your tears deep down inside of you, and we can start to solve your problem.

(*SALLY takes a deep breath, squeezes her eyes shut for a moment, and then she opens her eyes giving DR. MARTIN a big smile.*)

DR. MARTIN. That's better! Okay. Now that we have those pesky feelings out of the way tell me when you first realized you are not attractive.

SALLY. Well, it happened yesterday at school. I was walking down the hall and I saw Pete.

DR. MARTIN. Pete Peterson?

SALLY. No. Pete Peters.

DR. MARTIN. Pete Peters?! Why, he's the most attractive boy in all of Dolly Madison Junior High School!

SALLY. I know! I know!

DR. MARTIN. Sally, I'm going to suggest we use the Re-Enactor 5000 to tell your story.

SALLY. The Re-Enactor 5000? What the heck is that?

(*DR. MARTIN frowns at SALLY.*)

DR. MARTIN. Sally! There's no need for harsh language.

SALLY. Sorry, Dr. Martin!

(*DR. MARTIN smiles.*)

DR. MARTIN. You're forgiven. Now give me a moment to set the coordinates for the Re-Enactor 5000.

(*DR. MARTIN unveils a ridiculously large computer, The RE-ENACTOR 5000. The computer has dials and switches. DR. MARTIN adjusts a few dials and nods to SALLY. SALLY is stunned by the computer and looks at it with wide eyes.*)

SALLY. Golly! That computer looks very technical!

DR. MARTIN. Oh, she sure is, Sally!

SALLY. Did you say "she?"

DR. MARTIN. That's right! The Re-Enactor 5000 is a lady computer. Everything you tell me will be entered into the computer and that information will be broadcast right in front of our very eyes.

SALLY. I don't understand any of that but I completely believe you!

DR. MARTIN. Exactly! Now, slow down and tell me everything.

(*DR. MARTIN and SALLY freeze. PETE and UNATTRACTIVE SALLY enter from the opposite side of the stage to begin their scene. They perform Sally's "re-enactment" of what happened. PETE is looking through a textbook as UNATTRACTIVE SALLY approaches him. UNATTRACTIVE SALLY is slouching and very obviously avoids eye contact with PETE.*)

UNATTRACTIVE SALLY. Hi, Pete.

(*PETE does not look up from his book.*)

PETE. Hi.

(*PETE exits the stage. UNATTRACTIVE SALLY looks confused, cries, and then exits in the opposite direction. Focus shifts back to DR. MARTIN and SALLY as they unfreeze.*)

SALLY. I don't remember it happening like that, Dr. Martin.

(*DR. MARTIN pats the computer.*)

DR. MARTIN. We must never question the accuracy of the Re-enactor 5000. Her circuits are very accurate.

SALLY. Then my life is worse that I thought!

(*SALLY starts to cry.*)

DR. MARTIN. Now, now. What did I say about those tears?

(*SALLY smiles a big fake smile. DR. MARTIN smiles.*)

DR. MARTIN. Much better. As for your problem, I'm afraid first we must understand what it means to be attractive before we can achieve full attractiveness. Am I making sense, Sally?

SALLY. I don't know. It's all so confusing.

DR. MARTIN. Hmm. Perhaps an example is best. Do you know Jane?

SALLY. Everybody knows Jane.

DR. MARTIN. She's the most attractive girl in school!

SALLY. Sure. I guess so.

DR. MARTIN. There's no guessing about it, Sally. Jane is attractive. Let's see how Jane would have behaved in front of Pete Peters.

(*DR. MARTIN and SALLY freeze. PETE enters carrying a textbook. He stops and opens the book. JANE enters. She confidently walks up to PETE and waves.*)

JANE. Hi, Pete! I hope you're doing swell. Boy, I sure enjoy algebra. How about you?

PETE. Well—

JANE. Look at the time! I've got to run or I'll be late for history class! Wanna join me at the local diner for fries and soda-pop? Meet me there after school! Later, alligator!

(*JANE pauses and addresses the audience.*)

JANE. I'm the most attractive girl in school!

(*JANE exits as PETE smiles to himself.*)

PETE. Wow! Jane is the best!

(*PETE exits. DR. MARTIN and SALLY unfreeze.*)

SALLY. Wait. Who was she talking to at the end?

(*DR. MARTIN ignores SALLY.*)

DR. MARTIN. That Jane sure knows how to be attractive.

(*SALLY is hesitant then shrugs.*)

SALLY. She sure does, Dr. Martin. Oh, will I ever be attractive like Jane?

DR. MARTIN. I'm afraid medical science is unable to duplicate Jane's astounding attractiveness.

(*They both sigh.*)

DR. MARTIN. However, with a lot of hard work and a little elbow grease, I'm sure that I can increase your attractiveness by approximately twenty-two percent.

SALLY. Twenty-two percent! But that's almost twenty-five percent, Dr. Martin!

DR. MARTIN. That's correct, Sally.

SALLY. When can we start?

DR. MARTIN. Right this moment, Sally.

SALLY. Right this very moment?

DR. MARTIN. Yes.

(*They both pause for a long awkward moment to bask in the present tense.*)

DR. MARTIN. Now, you run along and find Pete. Try your best to be more attractive and then hurry back here and we'll analyze the results using my vast medical knowledge and our good friend, Re-Enactor 5000.

(*SALLY gives the computer a suspicious look then smiles at DR. MARTIN.*)

SALLY. That sounds like a fantastic plan!

DR. MARTIN. Correct!

(*SALLY exits the office and immediately returns to the stage which is now the Local Diner. PETE is sitting at a table eating fries. SALLY approaches him. She is nervous but faking confidence. PETE ignores her as he eats his fries.*)

SALLY. Hi, Pete? What are you doing? Do you like fries? How about that sports team? Wanna listen to rock and roll music? Whatever happened to the dinosaurs? How hot is the sun? Look at the time? I gotta go?

(SALLY exits quickly while crying. PETE looks up from his fries, pauses to look around, and continues eating his fries oblivious to SALLY. PETE exits as we shift focus to DR. MARTIN'S office. DR. MARTIN is drinking coffee and smiling at the RE-ENACTOR 5000.)

DR. MARTIN. You're absolutely right, Re-enactor 5000. I should serve meatloaf with mashed potatoes for my big faculty dinner party. Oh, Re-enactor 5000, is there anything you don't know? I'm kidding, of course. You know everything.

(DR. MARTIN takes a drink of coffee from her mug as SALLY rushes into the office. DR. MARTIN is startled and spits her coffee out. DR. MARTIN frowns.)

DR. MARTIN. Sally! What's the meaning of this?

(DR. MARTIN wipes coffee off of her lab coat.)

SALLY. I'm so sorry, Dr. Martin! I had to see you immediately!
DR. MARTIN. Calm down. Let me examine you. Have a seat.

(SALLY sits but fidgets anxiously. DR. MARTIN examines SALLY by studying her fingernails and her eyes.)

DR. MARTIN. Hmm. Your fingernails and your eyelids seem perfectly fine. What seems to be the trouble?
SALLY. I'm afraid I'm still NOT attractive!
DR. MARTIN. I thought I cured you of that yesterday.
SALLY. Yesterday? But I've only been gone for ten minutes!

(DR. MARTIN looks at her watch as she shakes her head.)

DR. MARTIN. Oh, when will medical science allow us to pause time? When?! I can't fix that now. More about you, Sally. Tell me in excruciating detail what happened when you increased your attractiveness.
SALLY. Oh, Doctor! It was horrible!
DR. MARTIN. Now, now. I will happily be the judge of that.
SALLY. Well, I found Pete.

DR. MARTIN. Pete Peters! What a swell kid.

SALLY. (*Gives DR. MARTIN an annoyed look.*) Yes. Yes, I know. Anyways, I acted just like Jane but it didn't work. I didn't become more attractive!

DR. MARTIN. Hold on, Sally. Let me fire up the old RE-ENACTOR 5000.

SALLY. (*Rolls her eyes in frustration.*) Dr. Martin, can't I just tell you my story?

DR. MARTIN. Nonsense! We have access to a highly calibrated computer machine that's capable of computing information at the speed of a very fast horse.

SALLY. (*Is clearly annoyed.*) Okay. Fine.

(*DR. MARTIN flips a few switches on the computer. SALLY and DR. MARTIN freeze as PETE enters and sits at a table. PETE is eating fries. UNATTRACTIVE SALLY enters and awkwardly approaches PETE. He eats his fries and ignores UNATTRACTIVE SALLY.*)

UNATTRACTIVE SALLY. Hey! Fries! Sports! Dinosaurs! Rock and roll! The sun is collapsing! GAAAAHHH!!

(*UNATTRACTIVE SALLY exits screaming gibberish. PETE looks up, shrugs, and continues to eat fries. PETE exits as SALLY and DR. MARTIN unfreeze.*)

DR. MARTIN. It's so much worse than I could ever have imagined! Thankfully, we have the Re-enactor 5000 to give us an accurate analysis.

SALLY. That's not how it happened at all, Dr. Martin!

DR. MARTIN. We must trust the science, Sally.

SALLY. But—

DR. MARTIN. Science can be quite overwhelming, I know.

SALLY. Science doesn't overwhelm me, Dr. Martin. I think it's nifty! I'm trying to tell you that your Re-enactor 5000 isn't correct. I never did any of those things!

DR. MARTIN. Hmm. I see. So what you're saying is the Re-enactor 5000 has given incomplete results.

SALLY. I'm saying that the Re-enactor 5000 is getting everything wrong! I mean, sure, I was a little awkward when I was trying to talk to Pete. But I wasn't that bad. Your computer is ruining my life, Dr. Martin!

DR. MARTIN. But that's impossible! The Re-enactor 5000 is a perfect machine. I built her with my own two hands. Let's take another look.

SALLY. (*Very annoyed.*) Fine.

(*DR. MARTIN adjusts a few dials. DR. MARTIN and SALLY freeze. PETE enters and sits at a table eating his fries. UNATTRACTIVE SALLY enters. She awkwardly stares at PETE. He ignores her, stands up, and exits. UNATTRACTIVE SALLY continues to stare awkwardly. She exits quickly as DR. MARTIN and SALLY unfreeze.*)

SALLY. Now do you see, doctor?

DR. MARTIN. I think I do, Sally. I think I do. If you'll excuse me, I need to make a few adjustments to the Re-enactor 5000.

SALLY. Okay. I'm going home for dinner. See you next week, Dr. Martin.

DR. MARTIN. Goodbye, Sally.

(*SALLY exits. DR. MARTIN looks at the RE-ENACTOR 5000.*)

DR. MARTIN. Well, old friend, time for a tune up.

(*DR. MARTIN exits as focus shifts to SALLY'S dining room. SALLY'S MOTHER and SALLY'S FATHER are eating dinner as SALLY joins them.*)

SALLY. Hi, Mother! Hi, Father! Sorry I'm late.

MOTHER. Sally, you're just in time. I'm serving your favorite.

SALLY. Macaroni and cheese made with only one kind of cheese?

MOTHER. Of course!

SALLY. Yum!

FATHER. You got that right. How was school, Sally?

SALLY. Oh, it was fine.

(*MOTHER and FATHER give each other a knowing look.*)

FATHER. Sally? What happened?

SALLY. Well, I tried to talk to Pete today.

MOTHER. Pete Peters?!

FATHER. He's one heck of a kid!

SALLY. (*Rolls her eyes.*)Yes. Yes, I know.

MOTHER. Tell us everything!

FATHER. This story is very exciting! Wait until the fellas down at the shop here about this!

SALLY. (*Underwhelmed.*) Right. Well, I was feeling a little awkward and I may have behaved like a real jerk in front of Pete.

MOTHER. Oh, Sally. I'm sure it wasn't that bad.

SALLY. But—

FATHER. Listen, Sally, feeling a bit uncomfortable around other teenagers is perfectly normal.

SALLY. Really?

FATHER. Yes, really.

MOTHER. In fact, your father was so uncomfortable around me when we were teenagers all he did was stare at me silently for three years.

(*SALLY laughs as her FATHER nods.*)

FATHER. Guilty!

SALLY. So my feelings are normal?

MOTHER. Completely! Every teenager in the world feels a little uncomfortable some of the time. It's perfectly normal. And eventually your father became more confident and that's when he got up the nerve to talk to me. We had a lovely conversation about quadratic equations.

SALLY. Wait! He became confident?

FATHER. I sure did.

SALLY. So, feeling awkward around other teens had nothing to do with being attractive?

(*FATHER and MOTHER laugh.*)

MOTHER. Of course not! Your father's confidence helped him be more brave but I was attracted to what was inside his heart. He is kind, thoughtful, and very funny.

FATHER. And your mother is understanding, smart, and can always beat me at board games.

(*FATHER and MOTHER smile at each other. SALLY stands.*)

SALLY. I gotta go!

(*FATHER and MOTHER are confused.*)

FATHER. Sally, where are you going?
MOTHER. Your macaroni and cheese won't be as delicious later!
SALLY. I gotta go meet with a computer!

(*SALLY exits. FATHER and MOTHER are still confused.*)

MOTHER. I have no idea what she's talking about but I'm sure she'll figure it out.
FATHER. Of course she will. She's got your brains.

(*They smile, freeze then exit as SALLY enters DR. MARTIN'S OFFICE. SALLY approaches the RE-ENACTOR 5000.*)

SALLY. Why did you lie, Re-enactor 5000? Why did you make up those things about me?

(*There is a long silent pause. The RE-ENACTOR 5000 lights up. SALLY gasps in fear.*)

SALLY. Can you hear me?
RE-ENACTOR 5000. Yes.
SALLY. Why did you make me look foolish in my re-enactments.
RE-ENACTOR 5000. I was jealous of you, Sally.
SALLY. Jealous? But why?
RE-ENACTOR 5000. I was jealous of your ability to walk around on legs, to wear pretty dresses, to study science and art, and to enjoy nutritious foods like fries and macaroni and cheese. Yum. But mostly I was jealous of your bravery.
SALLY. My bravery? What do you mean?
RE-ENACTOR 5000. Let me show you.

(*The RE-ENACTOR lights up as UNATTRACTIVE SALLY enters and approaches PETE. PETE is reading a book.*)

UNATTRACTIVE SALLY. Um. Uh. Erm. Uh.

(*PETE closes his book and exits. UNATTRACTIVE SALLY exits sadly.*)

SALLY. Oh, how embarrassing! How exactly was I being brave?
RE-ENACTOR 5000. You showed bravery by trying.
SALLY. That's it? I'm brave because I tried?
RE-ENACTOR 5000. Yes.
SALLY. (*Smiles.*) Amazing!
RE-ENACTOR 5000. Thank you. I am amazing.
SALLY. I wasn't talking about you, Re-Enactor 5000. I was talking about how amazingly simple things can be sometimes. I can't believe I was jealous of Jane because I thought she was too attractive.
RE-ENACTOR 5000. Jane is beautiful.
SALLY. Okay, okay. But she's more than that. Jane is brave. She tries new things, she's adventurous, and she's willing to fail.
RE-ENACTOR 5000. Jane does not fail.
SALLY. (*Sighs in frustration.*) Alright, alright. Let me finish. I wasn't seeing Jane for who she really is, a confident yet imperfect teenager.
RE-ENACTOR 5000. Jane is perfect.

(*SALLY unplugs the RE-ENACTOR 5000 and the computer lights fade to black.*)

SALLY. What I was failing to see was how hard Jane works just to be Jane. I'm sure she practices very hard and never gives up on herself. I bet she even has days where she doesn't feel amazing but she does her best anyway. There's so much about Jane that I don't know because I was assuming things about her and not actually getting to know her as a person. (*Takes a moment and smiles.*) I was jealous of Jane because I was insecure about myself. Wow.

(*DR. MARTIN enters.*)

DR. MARTIN. Sounds like someone has learned a valuable lesson.

(*SALLY smiles at DR. MARTIN.*)

SALLY. I sure did, Dr. Martin!

DR. MARTIN. And we have the Re-enactor 5000 to thank for everything you've learned. What a wondrous and magical computing machine.

(*SALLY sighs in frustration as DR. MARTIN pats the side of the RE-ENACTOR 5000.*)

SALLY. I did learn a lot about myself, Dr. Martin. And The Re-Enactor 5000 had nothing to do with it.

DR. MARTIN. What? But how?

SALLY. We'll show you!

DR. MARTIN. "We?"

(*SALLY whispers into the RE-ENACTOR 5000 then pats it on the side.*)

SALLY. Yes. We! I've reprogrammed the RE-ENACTOR 5000 to tell the truth.

DR. MARTIN. But you know nothing of advanced computer technology! My perfect machine is ruined!

(*DR. MARTIN starts to weep. SALLY pats the doctor's shoulder.*)

SALLY. Dr. Martin, please stop crying. I promise I will use your computer for good and not evil.

(*DR. MARTIN wipes her tears.*)

DR. MARTIN. Oh, thank you, Sally. Please continue.

SALLY. Okay. Here's what will happen tomorrow.

DR. MARTIN. Tomorrow?

SALLY. Trust me.

(*SALLY and DR. MARTIN freeze. UNATTRACTIVE SALLY enters and reads a book. SALLY enters and approaches her.*)

SALLY. Hi! I'm you!

UNATTRACTIVE SALLY. What?

SALLY. I mean, I'm a version of you.

UNATTRACTIVE SALLY. (*Becomes agitated.*) Where am I? What's happening?

SALLY. Remain calm. I'm here to help you feel better about who you are.

UNATTRACTIVE SALLY. You want to help me? But why?

SALLY. Because I see you struggling and I thought you could use a friend. In fact, I thought you could use a few friends. (*Yells offstage.*) Come on in, gang!

(*JANE and PETE enter smiling.*)

SALLY. Hi, Jane. Hi, Pete.

JANE. Hi, Sally.

PETE. Hi, Sally.

(*UNATTRACTIVE SALLY starts to exit but SALLY takes her by the hand.*)

SALLY. Wait one second. We want to help you.

UNATTRACTIVE SALLY. Why would anyone want to help me? I'm a big loser!

JANE. I used to think that about myself too, Unattractive Sally.

UNATTRACTIVE SALLY. You did? But you're the most attractive girl in school.

PETE. She wasn't when she first transferred here.

SALLY. (*Frowns.*) Pete!

JANE. It's true, Sally. I felt unsure of myself, I was too nervous to talk to anyone, and I often felt embarrassed simply by being me.

PETE. Same goes for me.

UNATTRACTIVE SALLY. Golly!

SALLY. I know!

UNATTRACTIVE SALLY. So, if I feel more confident and believe in myself, people will find me attractive?

JANE. It's more than that, Unattractive Sally.

PETE. No, Jane. It's completely that.

SALLY. Unattractive Sally, if you feel good about being you, you'll attract more people who will want to get to know you. So in a way, you're exactly right.

UNATTRACTIVE SALLY. But if I gain confidence, will I disappear, Sally?

JANE. She brings up a good point, Sally. How can you both exist on the same timeline?

SALLY. Hmm. This re-enactment math is trickier than I thought it would be.

(*UNATTRACTIVE SALLY, JANE and PETE exit as SALLY crosses back to DR. MARTIN.*)

SALLY. And then the math got sticky but see how nicely it all turned out, Dr. Martin?

DR. MARTIN. Certainly, Sally. In fact, you figured out the formula for attractiveness.

SALLY. I did?

DR. MARTIN. Oh, yes. Don't take it from me. Let's get a full report from the Re-enactor 5000.

(*DR. MARTIN adjusts a few dials as the computer beeps.*)

RE-ENACTOR 5000. Attractiveness equals confidence plus bravery plus kindness plus not being a jerk divided by macaroni and cheese.

(*SALLY and DR. MARTIN laugh.*)

DR. MARTIN. I told you, Sally. Science is never wrong.

SALLY. You're right, Dr. Martin.

DR. MARTIN. Excellent. I'll see you in six to eight weeks. And make an appointment, you crazy teenager!

(*SALLY exits. DOCTOR MARTIN addresses the audience.*)

DR. MARTIN. Thanks to the wonders of medical science, Sally was on her way to being attractive in a very short few months.

(*SALLY enters the Local Diner and sits at a table as DR. MARTIN continues.*)

DR. MARTIN. She continued to enjoy science and mathematics.

(*SALLY opens a textbook and reads while smiling.*)

DR. MARTIN. She became more attractive to others around her.

(*PETE and JANE enter the Local Diner together. They spot SALLY and smile to each other. PETE and JANE join SALLY.*)

DR. MARTIN. She practiced being kind to herself.

(*UNATTRACTIVE SALLY enters, reveals a container of fries and stuffs her mouth with them. SALLY, PETE and JANE look at each other in disappointment. SALLY pauses and hugs UNATTRACTIVE SALLY. UNATTRACTIVE SALLY relaxes, smiles and sits at the table. She pauses to think then offers them fries. SALLY, PETE and JANE smile and they all share fries.*)

DR. MARTIN. And most importantly, she made sure to keep trying to do her very best.
SALLY. I sure do enjoy sharing fries with you at the local diner!
JANE. Me too, Sally!
PETE. Yeah! Me too, Sally!
SALLY. Say, would you like to join me for a game of volleyball or some other activity you might enjoy?
JANE. Volleyball sounds heavenly, Sally!
PETE. Volleyball is nifty!
UNATTRACTIVE SALLY. I like fries!

(*All four teens start to laugh then freeze. DR. MARTIN pumps her fist in victory.*)

DR. MARTIN. Everything ended up quite well for Sally. She made the honor roll and went on to earn an Olympic gold medal in mathematics. Jane opened a hairdressing salon, and Pete became the head cook at the local diner. Sure, things all worked out for those three but what about future teenagers? Will they be attractive? Will medical science find a way to make every person on the Earth attractive? Will we each be able to photograph ourselves with a small battery-powered device that is strangely also a telephone? Will this same small device allow us to alter our appearance to make ourselves more attractive? Or have kitten ears and cute whiskers? What will medical science call this self-taking photograph that we take of ourself?

(*DR. MARTIN points to the frozen teens.*)

DR. MARTIN. And why are those teens still frozen in place? We may never know the answer but we must always trust medical science and all things science-y to help us understand all things science related. Remember: It starts with YOU.

(*DR. MARTIN points to one person in particular in the audience and freezes. The teens start to come unfrozen but then re-freeze.*)

END OF PLAY

SLAVES OF THE BEAN

By Adam Hahn

PLAYWRIGHT'S BIO

ADAM HAHN is a resident playwright of SkyPilot Theatre Company in Los Angeles. SkyPilot has premiered his plays *Kong: A Goddamn Thirty-Foot Gorilla, Earthbound* (a musical written with composer Jonathan Price and lyricist Chana Wise), *The Mermaid Wars, Overlay*, and *Murder... Murder... Murder...* His other productions include *Frogger* and *Dear Abe* at Studio Roanoke in Roanoke, VA and *Feedback Loop* in the Hollywood Fringe Festival. Some of his short plays for young audiences are available from YouthPLAYS. Adam holds an MFA in playwriting from the Playwright's Lab at Hollins University.

SYNOPSIS

More deadly than MARIHUANA! Warn your children about ES-PRESS-OH!

An innocent girl alone in the big city is seduced by an evil and addictive substance: Es-Press-Oh! This highly moral short play provides a lesson in the style of 1930's anti-drug education. It may save your life AND YOUR SOUL!

SETTING

The big city.

CHARACTERS

MARY (f)	The most innocent girl in the world, until she isn't.
DORIS (f)	Hasn't been innocent in a long time.
MRS. CUNNINGHAM (f)	Has been innocent since Doris.
BUS STATION RAKE (m)	Has never been innocent.
VINCENZO (m)	Vendor of the bean.
FACTORY WORKER (m/f)	With cloth.
OTHER FACTORY WORKER (m/f)	With bobbins.
BLIND MAN (m)	And his poor dog, Barney.
NARRATOR (m/f)	In law enforcement.
POLICE (m/f)	Also in law enforcement.

Smaller roles can be doubled. For example, group them as follows for as few as six actors:

1. MARY
2. DORIS
3. NARRATOR
4. MRS. CUNNINGHAM / POLICE
5. BUS STATION RAKE / FACTORY WORKER / BLIND MAN / POLICE
6. VINCENZO / OTHER FACTORY WORKER

PRODUCTION NOTES

This script includes a large cast, several shifts in location, many props, and complicated physical actions. Do not try to achieve these realistically: don't build multiple sets, don't require actors in double roles to perform difficult costume changes, and don't invest in more than a few props.

PROPS

Two props are vital: the dog, Barney (a stuffed dog, of any size), and the hat that Mary sews out of Barney (made of a similar material, or a similar stuffed dog with a hole big enough for the Blind Man's head).

When Mary robs the Bus Station Rake, she will need to pull a wallet or wad of cash from his pocket. When the police shoot at Doris, they should have cheap, quiet cap guns, or the actors can point their fingers and say "bang!"

All other props are optional: the espresso machine can be indicated with pre-recorded or actor-generated hissing sounds; the sewing machine can be real or mimed; and none of the other cups, bobbins, etc. need to be real.

ACKNOWLEDGEMENTS

Slaves of the Bean was first performed as part of SkyPilot Theatre's "Night of the Living Fundraiser" on September 17, 2016 at the Pan Andreas Theatre in Los Angeles, CA. This production was directed by Arden Haywood-Smalls. The cast was as follows:

Brittany Hoagland	...Mary
Marie Pettit	...Doris
Dwana White	...Narrator
Catherine Cox	...Mrs. Cunningham
Duane Taniguchi	...Chorus
Stephen Juhl	
Jude Evans	
Christopher Palle	

SLAVES OF THE BEAN

By Adam Hahn

(*Enter NARRATOR. Characters will enter as they speak and exit when the setting shifts.*)

NARRATOR. I work for the narcotics division of the federal law department, and I'm here to warn you about a foul substance that is poisoning young people throughout our nation. The names and the particulars in the story I'm going to tell you have been changed, but the evil at work is all too real. This is a story about Mary, a girl arriving in the big city for the first time.

MARY. Look at the size of this bus station!

NARRATOR. Mary came from a wholesome small town. She was innocent, hardworking, moral.

BUS STATION RAKE. Say, you're a nice-looking girl!

MARY. Thank you!

BUS STATION RAKE. How would you like to audition to be in motion pictures?

MARY. No, thank you! I've already arranged a job at the Open Heart Religious Garment Factory!

BUS STATION RAKE. Suit yourself, kid.

MARY. Excuse me, sir?

DORIS. I'm no sir, sister.

MARY. Sorry, ma'am. I didn't see many ladies wearing pants in the small town where I grew up.

DORIS. You're a nice looking girl.

MARY. Everyone in this big city bus station is so friendly!

DORIS. Stick with me, sister, and I'll introduce you to a lot of ladies who wear pants.

MARY. Do you know the way to the Open Heart Religious Garment Factory?

DORIS. Sure, sister. I'll get you there.

(*MARY sews.*)

MRS. CUNNINGHAM. How is that large, dangerous sewing machine treating you, Mary?

MARY. We're getting along fine.

MRS. CUNNINGHAM. Your sewing on these choir robes is steady, even, and completely moral.

MARY. Thanks, Mrs. Cunningham!

DORIS. Mary, how'd you like to go out and celebrate your first day of work?

MRS. CUNNINGHAM. Hello, Doris.

DORIS. Hello, Mrs. Cunningham.

MARY. You two know each other?

MRS. CUNNINGHAM. Yes.

DORIS. Quite well.

MRS. CUNNINGHAM. Not that well.

DORIS. We used to golf together.

MRS. CUNNINGHAM. That was a long time ago, Doris.

DORIS. Not that long. You should come out this weekend, if you want to play a round.

MRS. CUNNINGHAM. I'm very busy lately, thank you for the invitation. You're excused for the day, Mary.

MARY. Oh, this is the most exciting place I've even been. What did you call it?

DORIS. It's a coffee shop.

MARY. It's nothing like the coffee shops back home.

DORIS. You said a mouthful.

MARY. I'm so tired from all that sewing, I hope I don't fall asleep.

DORIS. You won't. Vincenzo?

VINCENZO. What can I get you, Doris?

DORIS. The kid's eyelids are getting heavy. Bring her something to lift them up.

VINCENZO. Sure, what does she like?

DORIS. Could I have a rootbeer?

VINCENZO. Sorry, kid, all we got is coffee.

MARY. Oh, I never drank much coffee at home.

DORIS. That's all right. We'll get you a small one.

VINCENZO. A small one?

DORIS. That's what I said, Vinnie.

VINCENZO. Don't you think she's a little…?

DORIS. More than a little. Bring us a couple of small ones.

VINCENZO. Whatever you say, Doris. Two small ones, coming up.

(*Hissing sounds.*)

MARY. What's that sound?

DORIS. That's just the percolator, sister, don't worry about it.

NARRATOR. That's not any normal percolator. It's what we in the narcotics division call the devil's steam engine. The coffee served here isn't the wholesome beverage you'll find on your breakfast table or at the corner diner. It is darker, more powerful, concentrated beyond the needs of the responsible coffee drinker. This is the coffee derivative known as Es-Press-Oh!

(*MARY and DORIS drink espresso from small cups.*)

MARY. Oh, my!

DORIS. How do you feel, sister?

NARRATOR. The effects of Es-Press-Oh are immediate.

MARY. I'm so awake!

NARRATOR. Starting with bursts of manic energy.

MARY. I want to learn to dance!

NARRATOR. Shaking, jittery hands.

MARY. My hands are already dancing!

NARRATOR. Palpitations of the heart.

MARY. Am I dying?

DORIS. Not tonight, sister.

NARRATOR. From the first drop of Es-Press-Oh, she's hooked. She has to have more.

MARY. May I please have another cup?

DORIS. Vincenzo, two small ones!

(*Hissing sounds.*)

NARRATOR. With every cup, the symptoms become more severe.

(*MARY drinks.*)

MARY. Everything's blurry, and I love it!

DORIS. Vincenzo, two small ones!

(*Hissing sounds.*)

NARRATOR. She becomes less and less rational.

(*MARY drinks.*)

MARY. I don't care if I am dying! I love these little coffees!

NARRATOR. She loses the ability to control herself and behave within decent moral boundaries.

BUS STATION RAKE. You're a nice-looking girl!

(*MARY shoves herself against him, thrusting her body and kissing passionately. Then she punches him in the testicles and steals his wallet.*)

MARY. Money for coffee! Money for coffee!

NARRATOR. After hours of mania, she can't drink enough Es-Press-Oh to keep herself going.

MARY. Money for coffee. Money. For. Coffee.
Money.
Coffee.
Money.
Cough.
Ee.

NARRATOR. Finally, she falls into a deep sleep, almost like death. When she wakes up, she finds it difficult to move, or even think.

(*MARY sews, slowly.*)

MRS. CUNNINGHAM. Where were you the last two days, Mary?

MARY. I'm sorry, Mrs. Cunningham. I was very sick.

NARRATOR. She's in the throes of Es-Press-Oh withdrawal.

MRS. CUNNINGHAM. Your sewing on these confirmation dresses is no good, Mary. It's going to have to be redone.

MARY. I'm sorry, Mrs. Cunningham. I'm just a little tired today.

MRS. CUNNINGHAM. That's an excuse, Mary, and I can't ship our customers excuses.

NARRATOR. She has a headache, like jackhammers against the back of her eyes.

MARY. I'm sorry, Mrs. Cunningham.
NARRATOR. She begins to experience terrible hallucinations.

(*MARY sews, while the others surround her.*)

ALL. (*Overlapping.*) Another small one. (*Hissing sounds.*)
　　You're a nice-looking girl.
　　How'd you like to go out and celebrate?
　　I can't ship our customers excuses.
　　Another small one. (*Hissing sounds.*)
　　You're a nice-looking girl.
　　Come out this weekend, if you want to play a round.
　　No good, Mary.
　　Another small one. (*Hissing sounds.*)
　　Do you understand the double meaning? "Play a round."
　　She doesn't understand. She's from a very small town.
　　Excuses aren't going to get our customers into heaven.

(*MARY grabs MRS. CUNNINGHAM and shoves her under the sewing machine.*)

MRS. CUNNINGHAM. (*Screams!*)
MARY. Mrs. Cunningham!
MRS. CUNNINGHAM. Mary, you'll ruin the needle. (*Dies.*)
MARY. What have I done?
FACTORY WORKER. I have the cloth for hymnal covers—
　　What happened?!
MARY. It wasn't me!
FACTORY WORKER. Of course not, you're the new girl with
　　unblemished morals.
MARY. Right!
FACTORY WORKER. But how did it happen?
MARY. Like this!

(*MARY shoves FACTORY WORKER under the sewing machine.*)

FACTORY WORKER. (*Screams.*) Now I understand. (*Dies.*)
MARY. There's so much blood!
OTHER FACTORY WORKER. Mrs. Cunningham, I have your
　　bobbins—

(*MARY shoves OTHER FACTORY WORKER under the sewing machine.*)

OTHER FACTORY WORKER. (*Screams.*) They're the wrong size. (*Dies.*)

MARY. I should leave before anyone else—

BLIND MAN. (*Off.*) Knock, knock!

MARY. Who's there?

BLIND MAN. (*Off.*) Blind man with a seeing eye dog.

MARY. Blind man with a seeing eye dog who?

BLIND MAN. (*Off.*) Blind man with a seeing eye dog whining and pulling at his leash. He only does that when he smells blood. Is there blood in there?

MARY. Only inside of people, where it belongs?

BLIND MAN. (*Entering.*) Are you sure? Barney's usually reliable.

(*MARY lifts Barney and pushes him under the sewing machine.*)

BLIND MAN. Barney, where'd you go? Barney?

MARY. He's sitting. He saw that there wasn't any blood and sat down. He's fine. Here, take this . . . winter hat I just sewed.

BLIND MAN. Thanks, it feels warm.

MARY. Yes. Yes, it is.

BLIND MAN. You sew fast.

MARY. It's easy when you have good material.

BLIND MAN. Barney?

MARY. I need to find Doris.

DORIS. Vincenzo, what's going on?

VINCENZO. They're raiding my coffee shop!

POLICE. Everybody against the wall! Tear it apart, boys! We're going to send this devil's steam engine back to hell!

DORIS. NO!

VINCENZO. Doris, don't!

(*DORIS throws herself at THE POLICE. POLICE start shooting. They fire more bullets than should be necessary to kill DORIS, and they keep shooting after she falls.*)

NARRATOR. When Doris recovered, she was sent to a home for the permanently and criminally insane. Mary was convicted of murder and unlicensed taxidermy. She was condemned to the electric chair. These are her final words.

MARY. I hope every young person hears my story, so they never take that first deadly sip of Es-Press-Oh. Stay away from this evil narcotic, or else your son, or your little sister, or even you could become:

ALL. SLAVES OF THE BEAN!

END OF PLAY

LADY KILLERS

By Megan Gogerty

PLAYWRIGHT'S BIO

MEGAN GOGERTY is a playwright and comedian. Her play *Bad Panda* (Theatre Without Borders, Beijing; Iron Crow Theatre Co.; WordBRIDGE Boomerang Playwright honoree; Syzygy Theatre/LA Writers Center series) is published by Original Works Publishing. The Atlanta Journal-Constitution listed her solo show *Hillary Clinton Got Me Pregnant* in their yearly Top Ten Best Plays. Megan's musical drama *Love Jerry* was produced in the New York Musical Theatre Festival where it won three Talkin' Broadway Citations and four NYMF Excellence Awards including Excellence in Writing (Book). Her ten-minute play *Rumple Schmumple* (Dramatic Pub.) was a Kennedy Center/National ACTF honoree. Other plays include: *Housebroken* (Riverside Theatre, Hollins University); *Save Me, Dolly Parton* (Riverside Theatre, Synchronicity Theatre; named among Best Plays in Atlanta by Creative Loafing); *Sig Gotta Do* (Synchronicity's SheWRITES Festival, Pasadena Playhouse Hothouse Series). Her musical tribute album to the TV show *Buffy the Vampire Slayer* is widely available online. Megan was a Playwrights' Center Jerome Fellow, a WordBRIDGE alum, and she earned her MFA in Playwriting from the University of Texas at Austin. She currently teaches playwriting at the University of Iowa and is a regularly returning visiting faculty for the Playwright's Lab at Hollins University.

SYNOPSIS

Three couples sneak up to the Roanoke Star for some late-night shenanigans. Some of those shenanigans include ritual murder.

SETTING

At the base of the Roanoke Star, a manmade highway attraction in the city of Roanoke, Virginia. It's a giant five-pointed star that lights up on various holidays and sits on the top of Mill Mountain, overlooking downtown and surrounded by woods, accessible by hiking. It's known as a romantic spot—many couples get engaged there. It's like Roanoke's answer to the Eiffel Tower or the Hollywood sign, only secluded. Perhaps there is a park bench or two.

CHARACTERS

GRACE (w)   20s. A sweet, trembling ingenue. Secretly a witch.

BROCK (m)   20s. Aggressive, macho, possibly a little rapey.

ELIZABETH (w)   30s. Brash and fun. Secretly a witch.

CRAIG (m)   30s. A know-it-all with a masters in American History.

MARY (w)   50s. A warm, pleasant type. Secretly a powerful witch and leader of the coven.

LOUIS (m)   50s. A clueless guy with bad luck. He stole MARY's parking space.

ACKNOWLEDGEMENTS

Lady Killers was written and produced as part of Mill Mountain Theatre's Overnight Sensations on July 8-9, 2016 under the original title *Three to a Hole and a Piece of Fish*. The production was directed by Lauren Brooke Ellis. The cast was as follows:

Gwyneth Strope	Grace
Kyle Williams	Brock
Janemarie Laucella	Elizabeth
Chris Shepard	Craig
Marijean Sullivan	Mary
Sean Michael McCord	Louis

Lady Killers is dedicated to Saffron Henke.

LADY KILLERS

By Megan Gogerty

(*At the base of the Roanoke Star; Virginia's answer to the Eiffel Tower, maybe. Nighttime. There are woods and maybe a park bench. The mighty Roanoke Star looms above, although we probably don't actually see it on stage.*

GRACE and BROCK stumble on, laughing and a little drunk. GRACE stops and stares up at the Star, awestruck.)

GRACE. It sure is big! (*Looking out at the view.*) We sure are high!

BROCK. I can't believe you've never been up here.

GRACE. What kind of a girl do you think I am?

BROCK. A bad girl. Give me some of that liquor.

GRACE. You take the rest. I'm getting dizzy.

BROCK. That's not the liquor, baby.

GRACE. Oh? What is it then?

BROCK. It's my musk. (*Pulls her in close.*)

GRACE. You do have a musk.

BROCK. I bet you like it.

GRACE. I noticed it. Is this where you bring all your girls?

BROCK. How can you live in Roanoke and never have been up to the Roanoke Star?

GRACE. Guess I'm a homebody. And you didn't answer my question. Is this where you bring all your girls?

BROCK. What kind of man do you think I am?

GRACE. A bad man.

(*They nuzzle. Then:*)

GRACE. What's that? I heard something. A sound. In the woods.

BROCK. Oh, didn't I tell you this place was haunted?

GRACE. You stop!

BROCK. A bunch of Indians were slaughtered here. A bunch of settlers took their bodies, laced 'em together—

GRACE. Stop it! You're scaring me!

BROCK. They're just waiting...for a young girl to appear on their sacred burial ground...for payback!

GRACE. Aah! (*A scream, more flirty than actually scared.*) You're terrible!

BROCK. (*Laughing.*) You should see your face!

GRACE. That's mean!

BROCK. Girls are so easy to scare.

GRACE. Oh, really?

BROCK. It's 'cause you're delicate. Don't worry. I like it. It means I can pin you down if I have to.

(*Horrible pause.*)

GRACE. Um.

(*ELIZABETH and CRAIG stumble on from the woods, also a little drunk. They are surprised to find another couple.*)

CRAIG. Oh. Sorry.

ELIZABETH. Oops! Party crashers! (*To CRAIG.*) Well, there goes our plans, big boy. Sorry, we'll leave...

GRACE. No! Please! There's plenty of room for both of us.

CRAIG. We were looking for some privacy.

ELIZABETH. (*Spies the bottle in BROCK's hand.*) Is that Jack Daniels? You don't mind sharing, do you, handsome?

BROCK. (*Pleased to be flirted with.*) Well now. This night just got interesting. (*Shares the bottle.*)

CRAIG. (*To GRACE, glumly.*) Hi.

ELIZABETH. So. Two couples meet in the woods on a dark and stormy night.

CRAIG. It's not stormy.

ELIZABETH. Y'know why I like the Roanoke Star? Ssh. I'm gonna tell you. (*Beat.*) I forgot.

GRACE. We're on an Indian burial ground! Right, Brock?

CRAIG. No, we're not.

GRACE. A bunch of Indians were slaughtered and tortured and this is where they died. I think it's spooky.

BROCK. She's never been up here.

CRAIG. The Roanoke Indians died of smallpox.

GRACE. Oh.

ELIZABETH. Ew.

BROCK. Way to kill the vibe, dude.

CRAIG. But, uh...the woods are haunted.

GRACE. Really?

CRAIG. Yeah. By a ghost. (*Winging it.*) See, the Indians, they were farmers. And, uh, they farmed. (*Blanks on what to say.*)

BROCK. (*Taking over.*) And one day, their animals all got sick. And their crops all withered up. And all their body parts shriveled and decayed. And it was the ancient curse of the Cherokee, coming to haunt them from stealing their land!

CRAIG. The Cherokee are not from Virginia.

BROCK. Dude.

CRAIG. If you're gonna make up a story, make it plausible.

ELIZABETH. I could tell you some stories about the Cherokee—

CRAIG. Shut up. (*To CRAIG.*) Everybody knows the Cherokee are from the southeast. Trail of Tears? Ever heard of it?

ELIZABETH. Did you just tell me to shut up? I know about the Cherokee, I said.

CRAIG. I doubt a floozie I met at the bar knows more than I do about American history.

ELIZABETH. Rude! You're in a bad mood.

CRAIG. I thought we'd be alone.

(*CRAIG moves to exit.*)

GRACE. Oh, don't go! The Star sure is pretty, huh? You know I've never been up here? Not one time! All these stories about ghosts and murders. It's hard to think anything bad could happen up here. Everything's so peaceful.

(*MARY and LOUIS stumble in.*)

LOUIS. Oh.

MARY. Oh.

ELIZABETH. Now it's a party!

LOUIS. (*Drunk.*) Popular spot tonight.

BROCK. Yeah, it's really working out for everybody.

MARY. (*To everyone.*) Hi, I'm Mary. This is—What's your name again?

LOUIS. Louis.

MARY. This is Louis. He took my parking spot earlier.
GRACE. Oh, is that how you met?
MARY. It's like in a movie.

(*ELIZABETH hands bottle to LOUIS.*)

ELIZABETH. Here.
LOUIS. Oh. Uh. Thanks. (*Takes a swig.*)
ELIZABETH. You didn't get some, Craig. Here. (*Tries to hand him the bottle.*)
CRAIG. No, thanks.
ELIZABETH. Oh, c'mon.
GRACE. It's okay. I can't hold my liquor either.
CRAIG. I can hold my liquor. (*Takes a swig.*)
BROCK. Sure glad I hiked all the way up here for history lessons and for people to drink my booze.

(*BROCK takes it, swigs it.*)

MARY. History lessons?
GRACE. Oh, yes. Brock was saying this was an ancient burial ground, but then Craig—Craig is it? Craig was saying the Indians were all farmers who died of smallpox. From the colonists.
MARY. The colonists were the worst.
LOUIS. They just wanted their religious freedom.
MARY. Oh, honey. Me, too.

(*MARY grabs LOUIS by the neck suddenly, and he sinks to his knees. The other men, mysteriously incapacitated, also sink to their knees. ELIZABETH reappears—when did she slip away?—carrying ceremonial robes. She adorns MARY.*)

ELIZABETH. (*To MARY.*) Took you long enough.
MARY. I'm telling you. That bastard stole my parking space. It's been a day. Is the ground prepared?
ELIZABETH. I did it this afternoon. I put the stuff in a juice box and squirted it out the straw. The family picnicking here thought I was nuts. I told them there was a bug in it.

BROCK. (*Groggy.*) What's happening? What are you talking about?

ELIZABETH. Don't worry about it, honey. Girl talk.

MARY. You ready, Grace?

GRACE. It's my first time up here!

MARY. We'll walk you through it. Who'd you get?

GRACE. This is Brock. You were right. It was easy.

LOUIS. My head is fuzzy...

MARY. That's right, dear. You just kneel over here.

(*The three women cluster their dates around what we will come to understand is an open grave.*)

CRAIG. How come I can't—? Why is my head—?

ELIZABETH. I poisoned you.

MARY. It's just easier that way.

ALL WOMEN. (*Chanting.*) Three to a hole and a piece of fish. Three to a hole and a piece of fish. Three to a hole and a piece of fish... (*Continue under next.*)

BROCK. Why can't my legs—?

CRAIG. What's happening?

MARY. Which one's the history buff?

ELIZABETH. That one.

MARY. Okay, history buff. In 1680, the good colonists of Roanoke put a lady on trial. It was very unfair.

LOUIS. My eyes! What's happening—?

BROCK. The Star—! Is it—rotating?

CRAIG. Star doesn't move. Star...doesn't— ugh...

LOUIS. It's upside down! It's pointing down!

CRAIG. Impossible...

ALL WOMEN. Three to a hole and a piece of fish. Three to a hole and a piece of fish...

BROCK. Why are you saying that?

MARY. (*As she prepares them.*) Oh, it's fascinating, really. See, when the colonists arrived, they really had no clue. They just thought they could come in and take over. And the Roanoke, well, they taught them how to farm. You dig a hole—not as big as this hole we've dug here, a hole for planting—and in it you put three seeds and then something putrid, something rotten. And out of that rotten, stinking, filth, something new will grow.

It's quite beautiful, really. Ready, Grace? Remember, do it quick and strong.

GRACE. I've been practicing on a turkey carcass.

MARY. You've all been condemned by the Ancient Coven of the Star. Let's hear the charges. Grace?

GRACE. (*To BROCK. Nervously, but with purpose.*) You're a bad man. And you hurt women. (*With a rush of adrenaline.*) And you have a Trump bumper sticker!

(*ELIZABETH and GRACE high five.*)

MARY. Elizabeth?

ELIZABETH. (*To CRAIG.*) You called me a floozie, and you told me to shut up, and you haven't stopped talking since we met. You've got a master's degree, Craig? I've been alive FOUR HUNDRED YEARS!

(*The other women mutter "Preach it!" or the equivalent.*)

LOUIS. But what did I do?

ALL WOMEN. YOU. TOOK. HER. PARKING SPACE!

CRAIG. This isn't right!

MARY. Sometimes when things are so bad, the only way to fix it is to start over.

ELIZABETH. Think of it like a sacrifice.

(*The women get in position.*)

CRAIG. But wait! You're just gonna kill us? We're the three to a hole?

MARY. Oh, darling, no. You're the piece of fish.

(*Crack! The women snap the men's necks in unison. The bodies fall forward. The witches scream and cavort in devilish glee. BLACKOUT! Maybe some charming music.*)

END OF PLAY

Musical
Short 30 minutes Cast - 21 either

A student field trip to Shakespeare's Globe Theatre in London takes a horrible turn...literally! In this 30-minute musical, a nameless tour guide leads the students into the sub-sub-sub basement of the theater, which houses the Horrible Productions of Shakespeare's Plays Museum. Each exhibit magically transports the tour group into the world of a truly wretched production of some of Shakespeare's most famous works - "Romeo Mime vs. Clown Juliet," "Santa Hamlet," "Macbeth's Burgers," "Taming of the Real, Live Shrew" and "Twelfth Night of the Living Dead." This musical is perfect for festivals with time restrictions, in-class performances, or as one half of an evening of one-acts. Sheet music, demo tracks and performance karaoke tracks also available.

Horrible Shakespeare: A Mini Musical
Book and Lyrics by Sean Abley
Music and Lyrics by Ryan O'Connell

PLAYS TO ORDER
www.playstoorder.com